MARY KAY
You Can Have It All

MARY KAY
You Can Have It All

Lifetime Wisdom from
America's Foremost Woman Entrepreneur

MARY KAY ASH

Prima Publishing

PRIMA PUBLISHING and colophon are trademarks
of Prima Communications, Inc.

Library of Congress Cataloging-in-Publication Data

Ash, Mary Kay.
Mary Kay you can have it all: lifetime wisdom from
America's foremost woman entrepreneur/Mary Kay Ash.
p.   cm.
Includes index.
ISBN 0-7615-0162-2
ISBN 0-7615-0647-0 (pbk.)
1. Success in business.   2. Success.   3. Women in business.   I. Title.
HF5386.A778 1995
650.1—dc20   95-12582
                                         CIP

96 97 98 99 00 01 HH 10 9 8 7 6 5 4 3 2 1
Printed in the United States of America

HOW TO ORDER

Single copies may be ordered from Prima Publishing, P.O. Box 1260BK, Rocklin, CA 95677; telephone (916) 632-4400. Quantity discounts are also available. On your letterhead, include information concerning the intended use of the books and the number of books you wish to purchase.

To every woman who is trying to balance the needs of her children, her husband, her home, and her career— *and finding it virtually impossible!*

Contents

Contents

Contents

Contents

Introduction

Back in 1981 when I penned my autobiography, *Mary Kay,* my original intent was to write this book. "But you can't write a book about priorities for women," several people in the publishing industry told me. "Old-fashioned values offend feminists. Today's women want to have it all, Mary Kay. They don't want to be told to prioritize."

Since that was my first venture into publishing, I listened to their advice. After all, their expertise was in books; mine was in working with people and cosmetics.

So I put the priorities book on hold and wrote *Mary Kay.* Now with more than one million copies in print, I've seen it published in a dozen or so languages. Later, in 1984, *Mary Kay on People Management* was released and it made *The New York Times* bestseller list. But I learned a long time ago that you can't rest on your laurels—"Nothing wilts faster than a laurel rested upon." Now, more than ten years later, I am writing what I initially planned to write.

I feel today's climate is right for a book about priorities for working women. Its message is needed even more today than it was in the early 1980s. Since my first book, tens of millions of women have entered the work force, and although opportunities for women are on the upswing, a host of new problems has arisen. Many working women are paying the high price of change. Their strong ambitions to climb the corporate ladder don't easily blend with their expectations of being ideal wives and moms.

Women's roles have changed more rapidly in the past decade than in any previous century. As a result, the average working woman experiences excruciating difficulty in setting her priorities.

To many women, the phrase *having it all* promises freedom. A popular dream for the American woman is to realize great achievement in her work while fulfilling her role as a wonderful wife, mother, and homemaker. Instead, career advancement adds responsibilities that demand more of her time, while her stress level shoots off the charts. Those who strive to have it all discover there are too few hours in the day to operate at peak performance in an arduous full-time job and, at the same time, tend to the needs of home, husband, and children. In their effort to emulate Superwoman, many women set incompatible goals which they naively hope to achieve simultaneously. This relentless pace means something has to give. *Priorities have to be established.*

My priorities have always been God first, family second, career third. I have found that when I put my life in this order, everything seems to work out. This is what we believe at Mary Kay Cosmetics. With trust in God, our firm has soared to astonishing heights in the business world, with annual sales approaching $2 billion at the retail level. God was my first priority early in my career when I was struggling to make ends meet; through the failures and successes I have experienced since then, my faith has remained unshaken.

Our belief in God should never be checked at the door when we punch a time clock. Faith is a 24-hour-a-day commitment. Many women have made the mistake of changing their beliefs to accommodate their work; it must be the other way around. No circumstance is so unusual that it demands a double standard or separates us from our faith.

This is a book about priorities that spring from good, old-fashioned values—the ones ingrained in our belief systems before the prevalence of drug use, violence, teen pregnancy, and a slew of other social issues. No matter how fast the world changes, exemplary values must remain constant. Women working to juggle the demands of career and family know the cost of success is high, sometimes too high. This is why it is so important to prioritize our lives.

When my company was founded in 1963, I knew it would be necessary to put my life with its increased responsibilities into proper perspective. To me, that meant putting God first, family second, and career third. Sometimes along the way, I wondered if everything would work out. Today, I can affirm that the growth and success of Mary Kay Cosmetics is a direct result of having taken God as our guide. I believe He blessed our company because its motivation is right. I want women to excel through the talents that God has given all of us.

A woman's family should be her second priority, also placed ahead of her career. After all, what value is professional success if family and personal happiness must be sacrificed? Remember, a career is a means to an end: you do well at your work to provide comfort and security for your family. It's important that we keep sight of what really matters in life. If we lose our families and our faith in the process of developing our careers, then we have failed.

Making God and family top priorities does not demean the role work plays in our lives. After all, where do we spend more of our waking hours than at work? Career may rank only third, but it is well ahead of a long list of other activities.

My purpose in writing this book is to assure today's working woman that she need not abandon her cherished values. If doing so were a prerequisite to her success, gains made in the workplace would be offset by personal losses. When she places God first, family second, and career third, good things are bound to follow. My goal is to help women to reevaluate their priorities, guiding them to take new—though old—paths toward a fuller, richer life.

chapter 1

LIVING BY THE
GOLDEN RULE

$\mathcal{A}$S YOU read this book you'll see that I put a lot of emphasis on how to treat people. The reason for this is simple. The real success of our personal lives and careers can best be measured by the relationships we have with the people most dear to us—our family, friends, and co-workers. If we fail in this aspect of our lives, no matter how vast our worldly possessions or how high on the corporate ladder we climb, we will have achieved very little.

With this in mind, each of us should have a philosophy about how we conduct ourselves with others. A long time ago I chose as my standard the Golden Rule: "Do unto others as you would have them do unto you." My mother taught me this creed when I was a little girl, and I have abided by it ever since. In fact, I wouldn't know how to live any other way. Some might consider the Golden Rule corny and old-fashioned, but no one can deny its simple truth. Imagine how much better our world would be if everyone lived by this creed.

The Golden Rule is not a spigot to be turned off and on according to convenience, despite the fact that many people apply it in some situations and discard it in others. As

Mahatma Gandhi said, "A person cannot do right in one department whilst attempting to do wrong in another department. Life is one indivisible whole."

When you believe in treating others as you would want to be treated, you should abide by the Golden Rule in your interactions with *everyone*. To treat people according to your whims on a particular day is not what this beautiful philosophy is all about. As we say in Texas, "That dog don't hunt."

THE GOLDEN RULE AS
A BUSINESS PHILOSOPHY

Many people draw the line on where and when to practice the Golden Rule. They may apply it at home, with neighbors, and at church or synagogue, but they leave it at the door when they go to work on Monday morning. Free enterprise's dog-eat-dog doctrine is their Holy Grail.

The creed of some businesspeople is *caveat emptor:* Let the buyer beware. This implies that there is no virtue in business, that it's acceptable to take advantage of the customer if you can get away with it. The buyer must always be on guard to get a fair deal.

It is no wonder that millions of hardworking Americans grew up believing that business is ruthless, and that in our highly competitive economic system, success comes only at someone else's expense. Some people think American commerce is fueled by heartless entrepreneurs and callous corporations, each with the objective of pounding their competition into the ground.

Understandably, those who entertain this hardened view of our free enterprise system are prone to abandon the Golden

Rule on the job. Otherwise they would feel vulnerable to the viciousness of their competitors.

Undoubtedly, some people will brand me a Pollyanna because I believe the Golden Rule has a place in the business world. In fact, I believe it not only has a place, it is a necessity. Before starting my own company, I spent many years working for someone else, so I experienced firsthand the distress a demanding employer can cause.

Before our doors opened for business, I vowed that no one associated with my company would ever be subjected to unfair treatment or unjust management. Mary Kay Cosmetics was founded on Friday, September 13, 1963. Since then, when a solution is needed for a people problem, I ask myself: "If I were this person, how would I want to be treated?" Today, with more than 375,000 beauty consultants who generate nearly $2 billion in retail sales each year, I'm convinced this philosophy works well.

There is every reason to believe that the Golden Rule will produce positive results in every company. Personally, working this way is what makes coming to the office every day worthwhile. If I had to take another route, it would have been better for me to have stayed retired back in 1963. Life is too short to live without the Golden Rule. It's as simple as that.

P & L MEANS PEOPLE AND LOVE

From day one, how people were treated at Mary Kay Cosmetics was more important to me than profits and losses. That's why I say, "P & L means *people* and *love*." Of course I'm concerned about profits and losses. I just don't give them top priority.

If you treat people right, they will work more efficiently and the profits will come in. Correspondingly, if you treat them abusively, their poor performance will be reflected in your bottom line.

The same advice applies to your customers. For good value and exceptional service, they will reward you with repeat business and by referring additional customers to you. But they will avoid poor products and inferior service like the plague. Doesn't this make sense? Being successful in business isn't a matter of taking advantage of people who need your products or services. On the contrary, it's a matter of giving them so much value, care, and attention, they would feel guilty even *thinking* about doing business with somebody else.

When you work with people, you must not have dollar signs in your eyes. If you are thinking, "How much money is in it for me?" the customer will read your mind. Your employees, customers, and clients will sense whether your interest in them is sincere. Insincerity creates an adversarial relationship—us-versus-them thinking. If a line is drawn between workers and management, or between customers and salespeople, people are put on their guard. In this hostile environment, any business will have difficulty growing.

My prime motivation for going into business was to help women. I wanted to provide opportunities for them to create better lives. I saw Mary Kay Cosmetics as a vehicle for women to realize their dreams. Our organization would supply the quality products, education, encouragement, and motivation women need to succeed.

Some people feel altruism in a company conflicts with the profit objective. Actually, the two are harmonious, because when your employees do well, they become content, enthusiastic, and loyal, resulting in a healthy bottom line. For the record, *profits* is not a dirty word. It's just that it should not be the only priority.

A STRENGTH, NOT A WEAKNESS

"Toughness" is considered a virtue in American corporate culture with good reason. The first settlers sent by King James I to colonize Virginia in 1606 were sponsored by a business venture, the Virginia Company, which later also founded the Plymouth Colony in Massachusetts. These courageous men and women were followed by other brave individuals who explored the American wilderness and forged a nation.

Trailblazers traveled west on wagon trains, and homesteaders staked claims to virgin farmland. They suffered enormous setbacks along the way, but they endured. This is our American heritage.

The pioneering spirit infuses our business culture. What was once a necessity for survival is now the American way. Being tough under certain circumstances is admirable; tenacity and perseverance are essential qualities for success in business. But there is much more to being successful. A hard-as-nails personality doesn't open doors in today's business environment. A person who lacks compassion is not an admirable leader. The railroad tycoons and oil barons may have amassed huge fortunes in the late 1800s and at the turn of the century, but as we approach the twenty-first century, a gentle, caring personality makes a more effective business leader.

It is a mistake to view benevolence as a weakness in business. Real strength entails being considerate and supportive of people's feelings. As the saying goes, you attract more bees with honey. . . .

IF I WERE IN HER SHOES . . .

When somebody comes to me with a problem, my immediate reaction is: "What would I want if I were in her shoes?" It's amazing what a different perspective you get when you put yourself in the other person's position.

In business, a little empathy goes a long way. At times it takes mental role playing to understand where somebody else is coming from. Then you can see what's really troubling him or her. To visualize how you'd feel if you were in somebody else's shoes takes effort. However, if you're in a managerial position, isn't this what effective management is all about?

Again, it's back to the Golden Rule—treating people as you would want them to treat you.

If you're in sales, putting yourself in the other person's shoes should be an automatic reaction. It will give you a better understanding of the customer's needs and help you respond appropriately when objections are raised.

Too many salespeople are thinking, "What's in it for me?" Instead of focusing on how closing the sale will benefit the customer, they're focusing on the commission they'll earn.

You have to think in terms of what's good for the other person. Learn to think this way reflexively in all dealings with people, and success will seek you out. No matter what you do for a living, this approach always works when sincerely applied.

REMEMBERING MY ROOTS

I have never forgotten where I came from, and this helps me empathize with others. As a little girl growing up in Houston, our family experienced some difficult times. I was seven years old when my daddy came home from a sanatorium, and while three years of treatment had arrested his tuberculosis, he was never able to work again. My mother worked fourteen-hour days as a restaurant manager, so I was in charge of preparing my dad's meals and taking care of him. With what women were paid back then, we constantly struggled to keep our heads above water. My most vivid childhood memories are of the hard times we endured. They keep me sensitive to other people's troubles and sorrows.

I can identify with a woman who comes into my office with personal problems because chances are, at some time over the years, I've been there, too. Whether there's an issue with her children or something isn't working in her marriage, I've had similar problems, and I'm able to understand how she feels.

Prior to starting Mary Kay Cosmetics, while working in direct selling for Stanley Home Products, I was a single working mother supporting three children. During some of this time, I was also going to college. So I know firsthand how a single working mother toils. I had to work long hours, and sometimes the only way I could find enough hours in the day to get everything done was to cut back on my sleep. Needless to say, there were mornings when I would have preferred staying in bed for an extra hour or two, but I forced myself to get up.

I also know what it's like to spend an entire day working, away from my family, and then come home late at night without a single order. I know the disappointment of working for weeks with a new salesperson only to have him or her quit for one of a dozen different reasons. During my decades in direct sales, I've seen just about everything imaginable, and I try never to forget these experiences. I want to be able to recall them so I can relate to another person's problems when she comes to me for guidance—or a shoulder to cry on.

The Mary Kay Cosmetics sales organization is structured so that everyone starts her independent career as a beauty consultant, learning how to use our products correctly and how to sell them. I firmly believe that you cannot teach what you do not know. It doesn't matter what an individual's background might be. We have women from all walks of life—secretaries, housewives, farmers, schoolteachers, nurses, and even some doctors, lawyers, and MBAs. We pride ourselves on being an egalitarian company. Every woman starts off the same way: Like everyone else, she buys the same demonstration showcase, receives the same basic sales information, purchases products at the same wholesale prices, and begins by conducting skin care classes. This way, when a woman works her way up to sales director and later to national sales director, she can understand the problems of the people in her organization. Why? *Because she's been there!*

I also know what it's like for the single working mother who works day and night to pay her current bills, put aside money for her children's education, and set something aside for the day she retires. I had my share of sleepless nights spent wondering how I'd take care of myself when I could no longer work because of my age. What would I do if I became disabled? If my income came to a halt for a few months, my meager savings would be wiped out.

Understanding that other women have the same worries inspired what is known today as our Family Security Program. It's a deluxe program for our national sales directors, the women who reach the height of achievement in our sales organization. In addition to generous disability benefits, it provides various retirement income schedules for national sales directors based on their age or years at that level of achievement.

For example, a national sales director who retires at sixty-five can receive an annual retirement income based on a percentage of her final average commissions, paid for a period of fifteen years. For our star national sales directors, this is a lot of security. Our top national sales director, who retired in 1995, for example, will receive an annual retirement income of over one-half million dollars for fifteen years. You won't find many major corporations that can match this plan.

THE INVISIBLE SIGN

God didn't have time to create a nobody—just a somebody. I believe that each of us has God-given talents within us waiting to be brought into fruition. Every person is unique and special.

It doesn't matter what people do for a living, how much money they have in the bank, or how they look. People are people, and everyone is important. I try to look for good qualities in everybody.

When I meet someone, I imagine her wearing an invisible sign that says, "Make me feel important!" The value of this is one of the most important lessons in dealing with people I have ever learned.

At Mary Kay Cosmetics, new employees quickly learn how much we value them. Each month, we hold a new employee orientation at which I personally welcome them into our family. I've been doing this since the company began; it's one of the real pleasures of my position as founder.

"We're like a giant wheel," I tell each group of new employees. "Each of us is a cog in that wheel, each has a different job to make that wheel go around, and each of us is important.

"If I don't do my job right, the wheel goes bumpity bump, and if you don't do your job right, the wheel goes bumpity bump. When we're all doing what we're supposed to do, the wheel turns smoothly and successfully.

"What if the air-conditioning breaks down?" I ask. "When this happens, the most important person in this company is not the CEO. It's the maintenance person, or whoever can make the air-conditioning work again."

Everyone wants to be appreciated, so if you appreciate someone, don't keep it a secret. You can always find ways to express your esteem. Fine deeds and performances are easy to recognize. For example, a sales manager might praise a top producer for opening a major account, establishing a new sales record, or winning back a customer from a competitor. It doesn't take much effort to appreciate outstanding performance.

Other times, however, you might have to look for things to appreciate. It is often easy to overlook a small achievement that is important to the person who did it. For example, you might say to your secretary, "It means a lot to me when you stay after five o'clock. You're not like so many people who, beginning at four-thirty, start watching the clock and make a beeline to the door at five every afternoon." Say this to your secretary the next time she stays late, and watch what happens. Chances are she'll relish your appreciation so much, she'll make it a habit to work past quitting time!

Get into the habit of expressing your appreciation to people, and observe how it affects them. In time, they will be performing over and above the call of duty because they enjoy the recognition.

Incidentally, I have told you how people respond to feeling important and appreciated, and how it is a tremendous method for motivating them. Yet motivation is not the primary reason I do it. How they respond is a bonus. I treat others this way because it comes from the heart. I believe everyone *is* important.

"YOU'RE GREAT!"

I think there's something wonderful about everyone, and whenever I get the opportunity to tell someone this, I do. It has such a positive effect on morale.

I always greet our employees with a warm, "Hi! How are you?" when I'm walking down the halls, riding the elevator, or going in and out of the building. When a new employee answers, "Uh, pretty good. How are you, Mary Kay?" I'll say, "You're not just good, *you're great!*" This generally gets a faint smile, and the next time I see him or her and ask, "How are you?" he or she will say, "I'm great." Each time afterward, the response is, "I'm great!" and the smile gets bigger and bigger. If you act enthusiastic, you *become* enthusiastic. And nothing is more contagious than enthusiasm—it spreads like wildfire!

When I attend a Mary Kay function at a hotel in another city, I generally don't enter through the lobby because it would take so long to stop and talk with the crowd of people there, the meeting would be delayed. For this reason, my security people usher me through the kitchen, where the dishwashers, buspersons, and other kitchen help are busy working. Within the hotel's employee pecking order, these people generally have the lowest status. But as far as I'm concerned, they're just as important as the hotel's top management, and I always greet them with a big, "Hi! How are you?"

It's sad, but so often they look at me as if they can't believe somebody actually spoke to them, and they nervously respond, "F-f-fine."

"No, you're great!"

"Oh!" they shyly say, "Th-thank you."

The next day, I might approach these same people and say, "Hi! How are you today?"

"I'm f-f-f—I'm great!" and big smiles appear on their faces.

"Good! I know you are!" I say back, and for the entire week that I'm in the hotel, this continues.

Once a hotel manager sent me a letter stating: "You did more for the morale of my people in just one week than I've been able to do in ten years!" His letter went on to describe how everyone's spirits were lifted. Isn't that great?

RESPECT FOR OTHERS

Some business executives put themselves in ivory towers. Because of their high rank in the corporation, they consider themselves better than their subordinates. Such an elitist attitude creates an adversarial relationship between management and employees. An us-versus-them attitude erodes morale, resulting in conflict and disharmony.

It's foolish for a company to treat employees at lower echelons as inferior. This kind of management only divides and never conquers, causing "us" to remain hostile to "them." "They" are seen as uncaring managers and never receive—nor do they deserve—loyalty from their workforce. In this environment, employees exert minimal effort—enough to keep their jobs but little more. They are not motivated to perform over and above the call of duty.

Being treated with respect is something every employee deserves, regardless of rank. Not only is it right, it has a positive effect on a company's overall success. When you show people you care for them, they return that care by working harder to see you succeed. As their team leader, they are rooting for your success—and they interpret your success as their success, too.

On the other hand, when they sense that your only interest in them is monetary and self-serving, they resent your success. In this situation, they may actually want you to fail even though your failure may harm them as well.

Years ago, extremely adversarial relationships existed between management and labor in the automotive and steel industries. Managers gave workers the message: "You are not paid to think. When you punch in each morning, check your brains at the door. Only management is authorized to think in this plant. Do only what we tell you to do. There is nothing you can tell us that we don't already know."

How would you react to this? Chances are, you wouldn't work enthusiastically. And whenever you came up with an idea to improve operations in the plant, you'd probably keep it to yourself. After all, you aren't being paid to think.

Now imagine working in an environment where you are treated with respect and told: "Nobody knows your job better than you do. The company wants your ideas on how we can improve. *We need your ideas.* Share them with us and we will listen. If we use your idea, you will be rewarded. And even if we don't use your idea this time, we will tell you our reason, so you'll know we welcome your *next* idea."

Wouldn't your response be much more positive under these circumstances? I know mine would.

It all boils down to: Respect begets respect. And isn't this what the Golden Rule is all about? It means treating people as you would want to be treated.

WHAT YOU ARE SPEAKS LOUDLY

You can talk about the Golden Rule and even incorporate it into your company's mission statement, but it's another thing to practice it day by day. A company whose actions don't match its words gives customers and employees bad vibrations.

You tread on thin ice when you only observe the Golden Rule halfway. We don't respect a minister who doesn't practice what he preaches or an elected politician who can't remember his campaign promises. Likewise, making conversation at the dinner table about shorting the IRS or evading speeding tickets with your new fuzz buster sets a poor example for your children. Don't let your actions invite mockery. In short, if you adopt the Golden Rule as your corporate or personal philosophy, do all you can to live up to it.

It takes more than words to live by the Golden Rule; it takes conviction. Schottensteins, an off-price department store in Columbus, Ohio, demonstrates this by its actions. Schottensteins is the largest retail operation in the world that is closed every Saturday—the busiest retailing day of the week. Its four large discount stores observe the Jewish Sabbath, just as its immigrant founder Ephraim Schottenstein did back in 1917 when he opened a tiny apparel shop. Today, Schottensteins is part of Value City Department Stores, a billion-dollar New York Stock Exchange company controlled by the Schottenstein family.

Ephraim's four sons took over the family business, and now grandson Jay Schottenstein, Value City's CEO, continues the family tradition, even though the store's several thousand employees, many of whom are not Jewish, could operate the business on Saturdays.

In today's highly competitive retail market, some say Schottensteins operates at a disadvantage: its competition finds Saturday afternoons immensely profitable. In the greater Columbus area, where the Jewish population is less than 2 percent, the Schottenstein family is admired for its convictions. The retailer's employees and customers receive the message that Schottensteins elevates principle over expediency. The company's honor is its most credible advertising.

To quote Abraham Lincoln, "What you do speaks so loudly I cannot hear what you say."

DO THE RIGHT THING

Doing the right thing goes beyond what the law requires. It's a matter of doing what you know is right. Former Supreme Court Justice Potter Stewart defined ethics as "knowing the difference between what you have a right to do and the right thing to do." This flies in the face of the belief that if it's legal, it's ethical.

For instance, you have the legal right to burn the U.S. flag, but I believe it is the wrong thing to do. Racial discrimination was legal at one time, but it has always been wrong.

As you can see, doing the right thing relies on personal interpretation. When external pressures are present, listen to your inner voice for guidance. When you are unsure about what is right and wrong, let the Golden Rule be your guide.

Still other times, difficult decisions that will be unpopular must be made. The CEO of a large company could decide to close a plant that is not turning a profit even though the lay-offs would devastate the local community's economy. A CEO has to look at the bigger picture. An unpopular decision could keep the entire company viable, averting harm to many other working communities. A compassionate and benevolent person is sometimes put in the position of causing stress to

15

others. Whether running a business or a family, this comes with the territory of leadership. Doing the right thing doesn't always mean doing the popular thing.

A CORPORATION WITH A CONSCIENCE

Henry David Thoreau put it beautifully when he said, "It is true enough said that a corporation has no conscience; but a corporation of conscientious men is a corporation with a conscience."

I agree with Thoreau that a corporation's conscience is only as good as the scruples of the women and men who run it. Many corporations work hard at doing the right thing. They try to be good corporate citizens who manufacture and distribute products and services of high quality and value; they try to operate by the Golden Rule. On the other hand, many corporations do not consist of conscientious men and women.

So what can you do? First, if you are seeking a job, I recommend you diligently do your homework to make sure you are allying yourself with a corporation that has a conscience. Begin by investigating the reputation of its top officers: Are they actively involved in the community? Does the company encourage its people to be active in the community? What worthy causes does the company support? What is its position on environmental issues? Are its products earth-friendly? What do its customers think about its products and services? Is it respected by its competitors? What do its suppliers and vendors think about the company? And, most importantly, how do its employees feel about the company? You might also want to check with former customers, suppliers, and employees. These can turn out to be your best sources.

16

Inquire about the company's principles and values. Many large companies have written mission statements, guiding principles, and/or values which they claim to live by. Companies that have published this information are never hesitant about sharing it with outsiders, especially a potential employee, so don't be bashful about requesting it. Once you have read it, ask employees, former employees, suppliers, customers, and competitors if the company practices what these principles preach.

Second, if you are an entrepreneur planning to start your own company, I can't think of a better place to begin than by operating your business by the Golden Rule. Make this a high priority; never make a decision that contradicts the Golden Rule.

Third, if you currently own or manage a company, institute the Golden Rule as a vital part of your business. This is not as difficult a task as you might imagine. A majority of people want to do the right thing, so if you assume a leadership role in this resolution, you will likely find many supporters.

I can say unequivocally that every decision we make at Mary Kay Cosmetics is based on the Golden Rule. We have done this so routinely that it's second nature to us today. In fact, we have a ritual at our national convention (which we refer to as "Seminar") that lets everyone know how we feel about working this way. When a director is promoted to national sales director, which is the highest level of achievement in our sales organization, she takes an oath before a packed audience of Mary Kay people at the Dallas convention center. In her new role as a national sales director, she vows to abide by the Golden Rule.

These vows are not idle words. At Mary Kay Cosmetics, they are how we live.

chapter 2

WHAT PRICE
SUCCESS?

*Y*OU HAVE always heard that people must pay a price for success. And it's true: hard work and sacrifice are necessary. But I believe the price is low in comparison to the price you pay for failure.

Some envious people insist that success ruins people, but I agree with Somerset Maugham, who said, "The common idea that success spoils people by making them vain, egotistical, and self-complacent is erroneous; on the contrary, it makes them, for the most part, humble, tolerant, and kind. Failure makes people bitter and cruel."

Of course, the secret is finding the level of success at which you and your family are happy and content. There is definitely a comfort zone, and moving too far beyond it can cause anxiety and stress. As I will discuss in this chapter, the sacrifice and time success requires may disrupt your personal life. You may discover that less success is more, in terms of quality of life for you and your family.

MY DEFINITION OF SUCCESS

Success is so personal that it's difficult to define. However, in order to discuss the price individuals pay for success, we need a working definition.

First of all, I don't think success can be defined in terms of financial gain. A dedicated schoolteacher, minister, or social worker, for example, may excel in his or her profession but never match the earnings of a professional athlete or entertainer. At best, monetary reward is a way for some people to keep score.

We all know of individuals worth millions of dollars who lead miserable lives. Many such people have failed in their marriages, raised spoiled children, and kept few or no friends. No matter how wealthy, this type of person does not have a successful life.

Just as money is not the criterion for success, living in poverty is not a badge of failure; one can succeed in personal aspects of life with little cash to spend. Of course, a certain amount of money is required to make ends meet. Abject poverty compounds problems while solving none. So financial security does contribute to happiness, but each individual must decide how much is necessary. Enjoyment obtained by accumulating wealth eventually reaches a point of diminishing returns. You can drive only one car at a time, wear one dress or suit at a time, and live in one house at a time.

Nor can success be measured strictly in terms of achievement. A novice golfer's successful round of golf would be a dismal showing to a scratch player. Countless other comparisons show that success is relative.

My definition of success would include living a balanced life. Balance means advancing your career up to, but not past, the point where it interferes with your happiness and relationships. Worthy advancement does not promote neglect of your husband and children. Nor should you work to the point where your health is endangered either physically or mentally.

Through it all, we must feel good about ourselves. We must not compromise our principles in order to further our careers. People who acquire immense wealth by driving themselves to the detriment of everyone close to them are not respected by themselves or others. What a boost to be able to like the person you see in the mirror each morning! At the end of the day, you can come home feeling good about what you gave to others, and you'll sleep more soundly at night in this knowledge.

So in defining success, a key element must be to have balance in your life. Smashing success in one area of involvement is canceled out by hopeless failure in another. For now, please accept my definition of success as maintaining balance. We will discuss this subject more thoroughly in chapter 3, "A Delicate Balancing Act."

WANTING IT ALL

In the 1980s, it was common to hear a woman proclaim, "I want to have it all." By this, she meant she wanted a successful career while being a wonderful wife and mother.

Wanting it all is an admirable goal, but some women run into trouble when they try to translate that dream into reality. Working women raise what seems like a reasonable question: If a man can put in a sixty-plus-hour work week and still be considered a good husband and father, why can't a woman do the same?

As much as I want women to have everything life has to offer, I recognize that we aren't like men in every respect.

Simply put, men do not have to face up to the challenges of motherhood. It is not possible for a woman to work sixty-plus-hour weeks *and* constantly be there for her children, making breakfast for them, taking them to school, and being home when they return in the afternoon.

Women with full-time careers must be creative about finding time for their children and their husbands. My assistant, Jennifer Cook, who has been with me for twenty-one years, is successfully raising a wonderful family while working full-time. While she cannot be there every day when her children come home from school, she does plan her schedule so that she never misses an important event in their lives. Jennifer has consistently found creative ways to provide for the needs of her family and to let her children know that they are important and special, such as tucking a personal note every day into their lunch boxes. She has learned to approach being a working mother with a positive attitude, helping her children see the fun and exciting events in their worlds rather than focusing on the time of separation as a negative.

"Being a family entails so much more than time spent together," explains Jennifer. "Some mothers can be with their children all day long and never have a positive influence on them. The most important heritage I can pass on to my children is a healthy self-esteem and a way of life in which they look for the good things. I've learned that people can rise above their circumstances, and being a working mother is a circumstance that can be handled with the right attitude. I am always willing to go the extra mile for my family."

Unlike Jennifer Cook, the challenges of "making it" in the business world cause some women to gradually distance themselves from their husbands and children. Whatever the reasons, bigger problems loom on the horizon if this situation is allowed to continue.

Women who want it all in the nineties must be realistic. Few careers offer women the flexibility to work and also spend as much time and energy with their families as they would like. I believe this is a major reason why business at Mary Kay Cosmetics has flourished in recent years. Women are attracted not only by the potential high earnings, but by the feasibility of arranging their careers around their husband's and children's activities. While being a Mary Kay beauty consultant is not for every woman, I recommend seeking out companies that offer similar advantages. Never forget, your family should always have priority over your work.

TRADE-OFFS

Recently I had an interesting conversation with Lisa, a thirty-six-year-old woman who has been practicing orthopedic surgery for three years. Lisa's husband, Craig, is a partner in a large accounting firm. He has been with the firm for twelve years, and his earnings have always been higher than hers. Lisa's income is now on the verge of taking off after her many years in medical school and as an intern.

"Craig wants to start a family," she confided, "just as I'm beginning to see my way clear of those student loans we've accumulated."

"Lisa, is that what you want?" I asked.

"Absolutely," she answered. "I want children very much, but it's a question of *when*."

She looked sternly at me. "All my life I've wanted to be a doctor, and finally, after so many years of hard work, my dream is coming true. But, Mary Kay, I've always wanted to be a mother, too. I thought if I worked hard enough, I could manage to be both. But the sixty-hour weeks I've been putting in don't leave me time to be the good mother I want to be."

Lisa is a fine surgeon, I thought to myself, and she would make a wonderful mother. What a shame this gifted woman is torn between career and motherhood.

"Male orthopedic surgeons don't go through this agony," Lisa sighed. "It just isn't fair, is it, Mary Kay?"

I sympathize with her, but there are no easy solutions. Lisa has to make a choice. She knows having a baby means putting her career on hold for a while.

I have warm wishes for every wife and mother who aspires to the status, success, and security of a career. Life typically doesn't let you have it all; generally, it requires compromise. The heavy demands of different roles make many women feel they must choose one goal at the expense of another. Oftentimes the decision means postponement, or even abandonment, of certain career ambitions.

Some women see this as an extreme sacrifice. For others, it's no contest; their families win hands down. What really matters to you? You can begin by asking yourself some serious questions about your career: Why are you driving yourself to succeed? Do you work to provide your family with security and a certain standard of living? Does your self-esteem hinge on your work—without it, do you feel inferior as a person? If you were to give up or postpone your career to take care of your children, would your family be better or worse off?

If you are married, some of your answers may depend on your husband's capacity to serve as the family's sole breadwinner. When a woman's earnings are essential to the family's financial survival, she doesn't have the option to stay home to care for small children, even if she prefers to be a nonworking mother.

If, out of choice or necessity, you are a mother who is a full-time career woman, be aware of the trade-offs that come with the territory. Your forty-plus-hour week at the office translates into less time with your husband and children. There are, after all, only so many hours in a day. You and your husband must juggle your time off so you can take turns being with the children, resulting in less time together as a family unit. Furthermore, even with today's modern man pitching in to help with household chores, the woman is generally responsible for the work around the house.

It's no easy matter for both husband and wife to work full-time and manage a family. A career that contributes to the family coffers demands a hefty price. Compromises are unavoidable.

NET GAINS

In the women's department of one of the finer stores in downtown Dallas, I was waited on by a mother of three. "I work three days a week while my two older children are in school," she confided. "A baby-sitter takes care of our little one."

I was curious. "Do you work here because you like to get out of the house?" I asked.

"No, it's because we need the extra money," she answered.

Considering her a potential recruit for Mary Kay Cosmetics, I asked her how much she made working part-time.

"I'm getting $10 an hour," she said. A smile appeared on her face when she added, "Plus, I get a 30 percent discount on the clothes I buy here."

I quickly calculated that her gross income was $150 a week. If payroll deductions were $30, she'd take home

$120—before expenses. It didn't take me long to figure out that if she bought many outfits, she'd be in the red at the end of the year. I didn't want to rain on her parade, so I took her name and passed it along to one of our sales directors who could show the light to this woman.

Before you choose between embarking on a full-time career and staying home with the children to run your household, take a careful look at your bottom line. Do you know exactly how much you'll net at your job after expenses?

Your many hidden expenses may include:

- Caring for small children: baby-sitters, day-care centers, or nannies.
- Housekeeping: You may have to hire part-time or full-time help.
- Transportation: public transportation or car depreciation, maintenance, and parking.
- Your wardrobe: Proper business attire is pricey, and the competition to "dress for success" is keen.
- Meals away from home. (Eating lunch out five days a week is not only expensive, it's fattening!)
- Miscellaneous expenses: hairstyling, manicures, makeup, drycleaning, and so on.
- Income taxes: federal, city, and state—which, depending on your tax bracket, could eat up in excess of 40 percent of your take-home pay.

Considering all these costs, how much will you actually net? Is this amount of money worth your working so many hours and being away from your family so long? And don't forget to consider wear and tear. I'm talking about the toll your schedule will take on *you*. Coming home dead tired after a forty-hour week only to make dinner, clean the bathrooms, and wash the clothes makes for an exhausting week!

MASTER OR SLAVE?

During the 1990s, record numbers of Americans are opting to start their own businesses. These fledgling entrepreneurs seek the independence that comes from being their own boss. To achieve their goals, they are willing to take substantial risks, and they are committed to working long, hard hours. My hat goes off to these daring businesspeople; they are the backbone of our free enterprise system.

Of course, it isn't all peaches and cream. While some will fulfill their dreams, others will endure living nightmares. Many will suffer severe financial setbacks, work long hours for low pay, and lose hard-earned savings that have taken a lifetime to accumulate.

A small-business entrepreneur pays a high price for success. For example, Sherril Steinman, one of our top sales directors, operated a flower shop in Pigeon, Michigan, prior to starting her career as a beauty consultant. A mother of two small sons, Sherril sought financial reward and independence but found instead that she had become a slave to her small floral business.

"I had no idea when I started my company that I was taking on an obligation that meant putting in sixty to seventy hours each week," she said, "oftentimes with no take-home pay."

Rather than enjoying the freedom of being her own boss, Sherril discovered she had no choice but to work extra hours. "It was a matter of survival," she explained. "If you're not there to do a funeral on a Saturday or Sunday, the funeral director will give his order to another flower shop. The same was true when I did weddings, which are almost always on weekends. As it turned out, I was working for my business rather than having it work for me. I was its captive, and I did whatever it required of me.

"It didn't matter if one of my sons had a basketball game on Friday night: if my wedding flowers came in on Thursday or Friday, I'd be at the shop until midnight each night until the big day came and went. After all, flowers are perishable, and I had a lot of money invested in them."

People who buy franchises frequently have the same troubles Sherril experienced with her flower business. In fact, many buy "jobs" that put them to work for longer hours and less pay—all for the sake of being self-employed! Shopping center leases commonly require tenants to be open seven days a week until nine or ten o'clock each night. Franchisers, too, often make similar demands on franchisees.

There are many other drawbacks to consider before starting a business. In addition to the long hours and financial risk, a small-business owner must pay exorbitant premiums for health insurance and a higher rate for Social Security. Moreover, there is always considerably more bookkeeping and record-keeping than you anticipate.

In summary, although it is true that you are your own boss when you possess your business, you may have to be a very tough boss to succeed—mostly tough on yourself.

BIOLOGICAL CLOCKS

Years ago, most women married and had children at a young age. Today, because a woman typically marries later and delays having children, the quiet ticking of her biological clock has become a deafening roar.

Many young, career-oriented women graduate from college qualified for management training positions in leading corporations. Today, graduate schools turn out as many women as men, qualified in fields such as medicine, law, and accounting.

In short, women are entering the professional world in record numbers, willing and ready to compete directly with men for leading positions.

These women are geared to ascend the corporate ladder, become partners in law and accounting firms, and go to the top of their fields. Given the opportunities, they compete on an even par with their male counterparts. With so much going for them, once they pick up momentum, they are driven to advance as high as their God-given talents permit.

But there's a catch. Unlike men, women have a limited time frame in which they can bear children. Women often delay starting a family, knowing it will sidetrack their careers. Some wait until their late thirties or early forties, when the risk of giving birth to an unhealthy infant is greater.

Losing the option of motherhood is not a problem for a woman who would rather not have children. But for a woman who wants children, it is tragic—and equally so for the woman who decides to remain childless but later changes her mind, after it is too late.

My advice to every young woman is to consider this issue carefully and make a definite commitment to her plan. Then she won't give up what may be the most precious gift God gives us.

EVALUATING YOUR PRIORITIES

I have a dynamic single friend named Betty who has always been ahead of her time. She started her career as a filing clerk, transferred to a low-level entry position in accounting, and went on to become one of her company's top managers. For a while, she was among the highest ranked women insurance executives in Houston. She retired last year.

Recently Betty and I were both seated at the head table at a women's conference. I made the mistake of asking her what she had been doing since her retirement.

"I was looking forward to my retirement," she responded, "but, frankly, now I'm absolutely miserable."

"But, Betty, you're a golfer, and you're active in the community," I said. "Surely, you must have more than enough to keep yourself busy."

"That's not the problem, Mary Kay. My career was my life," she confided. "I don't have children or grandchildren. In the office, I was surrounded by people, and in my high position, everyone always made a fuss over me. Even right after I retired, I had plenty of lunch dates and dinner parties to attend. But now that I'm no longer a bigwig insurance executive, I'm no longer on Houston's shortlist. After about six months of being away from the company, the phone just stopped ringing."

I saw tears in her pretty eyes. This was a side of Betty I had never experienced. "I made a big mistake when I chose to make my career the focal point in my life," she said. "I'm not saying I didn't enjoy the power and the recognition. But what do I have to show for it now? I knew all along I was passing up the traditional life by not having a husband and children. You know, not too many women did that back in those days, Mary Kay. But I rationalized, and felt proud of the perks of my career.

"Well, I had my priorities, and now I'm living with them," she concluded. "Boy, what I wouldn't give to be able to live my life over again."

To avoid having similar regrets, every so often ask yourself: "What is really important to me?" When you evaluate your priorities in life, chances are your career will take a backseat to your family.

Some women striving to climb the corporate ladder lose sight of what matters most in life. They put in more than sixty hours a week, take briefcases filled with documents home each night, and spend weekends thinking about the following week's work load. These women don't neglect their families intentionally; they just become overwhelmed by the demands of their careers.

We must not become so involved in our work that we lose what we cherish most: spending time with our husbands and watching our children grow up. We want to make certain our children become good people. Their early years are so important, and nobody can make the difference in their lives that you can.

We must not work so hard and long that at the end of the day we come home too exhausted to enjoy the friendship and love of our husbands. I see many women who are just too tired to care about this relationship. But, having a healthy relationship with your husband brings deeper happiness than winning a big promotion, a fancy title, or a higher salary.

So evaluate your priorities! In all likelihood, you put in those long working hours so you can afford to enhance your family's lifestyle and expand your children's opportunities. If your career diminishes your most precious relationships, it defeats its purpose. Perhaps spending less time on your career and more time with your dear ones will mean less financial success but more happiness overall.

It all boils down to this: What good is a successful career if you lose your husband and children in the process? With no one to share in the fruits of your labor, success has little meaning. Deprived of your family, all the money in the world won't buy you happiness.

chapter 3

A DELICATE BALANCING ACT

*W*EARING THE three hats of a full-time wife, mother, and career woman is no easy task. Depending upon your children's ages and the demands of your job, it can be formidable. And if you have an uncooperative husband to boot, you're really in for some rough times.

Today, millions of American women are wearing these three hats. Just a generation ago, it was rare to see a woman working full-time away from home while simultaneously looking after a family. Needless to say, the typical American family no longer resembles early television's "Ozzie and Harriet." At three o'clock you are unlikely to find today's Harriet Nelson rolling out cookie dough while she waits for Ricky and David to walk in the door.

Chances are your home life isn't much like "The Cosby Show" either. The parents on this sitcom, Clair and Cliff Huxtable, are professionals who seldom have a problem that can't be worked out perfectly in the course of a half-hour episode. Wouldn't it be nice if real life were like this?

The average American family finds that even two paychecks don't always make ends meet. Single working mothers—and sometimes married mothers whose husbands earn a steady income—have no choice about entering the job market. The high cost of living rules out staying home with the children.

This means a mother must now put in at least a forty-hour week at her "other" full-time job. Her main full-time job is taking care of her family. Even though she's away from home nine to ten hours each day, her work there doesn't cease. There are still meals to prepare, clothes to wash, and floors to mop. Every homemaker has sighed, "My day never ends."

To make it all work, a woman must walk that fine line that balances her career with her personal life. Balance doesn't just happen. A working mother must make a sustained effort to achieve and maintain it, because without a certain symmetry in her days, she is flirting with disaster.

SWITCHING GEARS

A woman's work at home and on the job are distinctly different. So great is the contrast that she must make a conscious transformation several times a day. Whether she works in sales, bookkeeping, office management, medicine, law, or accounting, her role as a wife and mother is unlike her paid job. She must make a mental adjustment in order to switch gears smoothly on her way to work each morning.

This transformation is rarely easy. Mom doesn't simply walk out the door, drive to work, and enter the office wearing her Ms. Career Woman hat. Although she may physically accomplish this, unless she finds a way to make the necessary mental transition as well, she might as well stay home.

To keep her work from suffering, a woman must be able to leave her personal problems at home. As much as possible, she must put pending issues with her husband and children on hold until day's end.

But circumstances sometimes arise during the workday that give her no choice but to switch gears and slip on her home-maker hat. On her lunch hour, she could perhaps tend to a family errand. Or maybe she'll receive an urgent call from her child's school. Afterward, when the personal matter is re-solved, she puts on her career hat again. For a woman in sales or one who works in her home, the changing of hats may occur several times during the course of a day.

The transition from office to home is even more troublesome. The occupations of America's millions of working mothers may run the gamut—from executive, supervisor, and surgeon to jobs that require little or no decision-making—but whether a woman's career is high-powered or toilsome has little bearing on her role as a wife and mother. If a man's home is his castle and hence he is king, in a woman's home, she is queen. She may very well also be cook, dishwasher, and chambermaid.

I have talked with many women about making that transi-tion from office to home, and I find their methods fascinating. For example, one acquaintance of mine—an executive with a reputation for being tough—plays her Bach CD collection in her car on the way home from the office. This allows her to unwind before seeing her family. Another listens to inspira-tional tapes, which is also my favorite way to make the transi-tion to and from my office. A friend on the West Coast simply concentrates on the scenery by taking an off-the-beaten-path route home. Many women in larger metropolitan areas catch up on their reading while riding the subway. And still others chat with a fellow commuter in the car, bus, or train. No mat-ter how you make the transition, what's important is to switch gears consciously so you don't charge into the house as the other you. Once you walk through that door, you must forget about being the district manager or the department head. At home you're "honey" and "Mom."

Regardless of what you do from nine to five, your family needs you to assume a leadership role at home. You may be a secretary, filing clerk, or assembly line worker who doesn't supervise anyone, but in your home, you're just as much the woman of the house as the female CEO of a large company is in her home. And just as she removes her work hat, so must you remove yours. The hand that gave a firm handshake at the office, and that gently rocked the cradle in the nursery, must now take up the scepter of leadership at home. You can't afford to walk in the door and drop into a chair; you have to take charge of your turf.

I acknowledge that many women are so exhausted by the end of their working day that they can hardly function. Nobody said being a working mother was a piece of cake.

MOTHERS WORKING ON OVERTIME

After a working mother gets home from her daytime job, she usually must put in several more hours of work before calling it a day. Typically, her first responsibility is to feed her family. Say, for example, she has arrived home and changed clothes by six o'clock. This doesn't allow much time to put dinner on the table because by now her restless brood has a healthy appetite. So the pressure is on. If she's efficient and the family pitches in, after cooking, eating, and cleaning up, she'll do well to be out of the kitchen by eight. This gives her an hour or so to do housework that can't wait, help the children with homework, and go through their bedtime routine. Little time remains for reading, watching television, or returning phone calls. And only after the children are asleep can she and her husband spend quiet time together.

As a result of these demands on their time, many women today operate on less sleep than they require. They may get up an hour or two early to do work they brought home from the office, prepare breakfast and lunch for their children, apply their makeup, and get dressed. Years ago, I heard somebody say that if you get up two and a half hours early three days a week, you add an extra day to your week. At the time, I had three young children and I wasn't able to accomplish what I needed to do in a seven-day week. So I decided to get up early *six* times a week and have a nine-day week. I discovered that working at five in the morning gave me the added bonus of not being bothered by telephone calls and other interruptions. This early-morning time has become the most productive part of my day, and I've been getting up at five ever since.

Over the years, when Mary Kay people asked how I manage to get so much done, I told them about rising early. Many of them decided to follow the same routine. Now I invite every new sales director in our company to join my Five O'clock Club. Today, the club has thousands of members.

Most working mothers catch up on their household chores during the weekends, but if they have small children, they may not find enough hours to get everything done. Furthermore, on Saturday and Sunday, a mother wants to enjoy activities that she couldn't do during the week. And every family should have—and treasure—recreational time together.

Even though a working mother's life sounds like drudgery, these years with your children should be the happiest of your life. It's a good thing this stage of life happens when you're young, healthy, and energetic, because it does take plenty of energy!

DON'T WASTE DOLLAR
TIME ON PENNY JOBS

I can't understand the way some highly paid female executives place so much value on their time at work and so little on their off-the-job time. If you work full days at the office and make a decent salary, you should hire a housekeeper to do the lion's share of your tedious housecleaning. Even if a maid service comes in only a day or two a week, it's money well spent to recoup leisure time with your family.

It's false economy to spend your precious time vacuuming carpets, cleaning windows, and ironing clothes when you can pay somebody else to do it for a fraction of what you earn each hour. Don't spend dollar time on penny jobs! Of course, if you really enjoy housework, then, by all means, do it. But if you find it dull and exhausting, hire someone and spend the new-found time with your husband and children.

Years ago, I gave this advice to a good friend, Dalene White, who joined Mary Kay Cosmetics on the very day we opened our doors. Dalene was as anxious as I was to get our little company off to a good start, so she hired a housekeeper who came in every Tuesday. This provided Dalene with more time and energy to devote to her new career.

"With my housekeeper," Dalene recalls, "I was able to do skin care classes and really concentrate on my work. I no longer had to worry about all the housekeeping that was waiting for me when I got home."

As an independent salesperson with her earnings based on sales instead of by the hour, she might have decided to do the housekeeping herself. But when the two of us sat down to calculate what her time was worth—dividing her weekly earnings by the hours she worked—Dalene was able to put a price tag on her time.

Sometime later, after Dalene's earnings had increased signif- icantly, I asked, "How often does your housekeeper come in?"

"Three days a week," she replied.

"Does this free your time so you don't have to bother with housework?"

"No, Mary Kay, I'm still spending too much time on it."

"Maybe you should hire full-time help," I suggested.

Dalene's housekeeper certainly paid off. Dalene went on to become one of our first two national sales directors and today has an income in the high six figures.

While Dalene liked the additional earnings that she gener- ated during her freed-up time, she especially appreciated the extra time she could spend with her husband and children. "Previously, my spare time was eaten up by housework," she says, "and removing that burden meant more quality time with my family."

PRIORITIZING

For a working mother to maintain balance in her life, she must have her priorities clearly laid out. Some women's careers take precedence over everything else in their lives. They are so anxious to succeed that their lives revolve around their work. These women put in long hours, bring home full brief- cases every night, and are on call around the clock, weekends included. Their families play second fiddle to their careers.

My family has always come before my career. My sole rea- son for working when my children were small was to provide for them. Had I been independently wealthy during those years, I would have stayed home with my family. I was hap- piest when I was with my children, but as a single parent, I didn't have a choice.

Since God and my family were my number one and number two priorities, I tried never to let my career get in the way. Whenever I had to make choices, my career took third place. If an important activity involving my children came up, I made sure I was there. Since I was a commissioned salesperson, my income depended upon my ability to work every day. Still, I gave up my earnings many times to attend priceless school plays and scout meetings.

All work and no play or time with her children is obviously wrong for any working mother. But if a woman's family depends on her earnings, she also must do her job, and she has a further responsibility not to let her employer down. A salaried employee owes a fair day's labor for a fair day's salary, even if she would prefer to spend her time with her children. To many innovative mothers, this obligation means finding ways to rearrange their working hours.

Women who are self-employed can rearrange their schedules more easily. Lane Nemeth, the founder and president of Discovery Toys Inc., says that her daughter, Tara, has always been her top priority. "Tara was only two when I began my company in the mid-1970s," Nemeth explains. "One prime reason for being in business for myself was to spend more time with my daughter. I felt that I had the choice to have or not have a child, and if I were going to have one, that child would be my number one priority for a certain number of years. After all, a child doesn't ask to be born."

In the beginning, Nemeth worked part-time on her new business; when her daughter entered first grade, Nemeth expanded her hours to work around her daughter's schedule. "I was home every single night by five, so it meant Tara was only with a sitter for two hours a day," Nemeth says. "However, if something came up that involved my daughter, I'd drop whatever I was doing to be with her. Once I abruptly left a meeting with my banker because Tara called and said she was having a problem. I simply excused myself, and I was gone."

In spite of putting her career behind her family, Lane Nemeth has succeeded in a grand way. Today, sales of Discovery Toys are approaching the $100-million mark.

Becoming a mother changes your life forever. Your responsibility to provide love and care for your child is a lifetime commitment. No matter how big and strong your child grows, you never stop being a mother. And, yes, especially when your child is small, you will make numerous personal sacrifices. But most mothers agree that such sacrifices enrich their lives.

FAMILY-FRIENDLY WORKPLACES

Many companies, sensitive to the special needs of working mothers, are investigating family-friendly policies. Some have even adjusted work hours so that mothers (and, in some cases, fathers) can attend to family matters without shirking the responsibilities of their jobs. For example, in California, companies are required by law to provide parental leave opportunities for employees with children participating in school functions.

Even so, with the realities of the corporate world in today's fast-changing economy, it will likely never be possible for a woman always to keep the demands of her career from interfering with the responsibilities of her family. A secretary's hours usually need to match her boss's schedule. A manager's hours may be dependent on schedules outside her control. So be aware, not every woman will be able to set her work hours according to what is ideal for her family. Choices will need to be made. However, only when your priorities are clear can these important choices be soundly made.

Undoubtedly, flexible schedules are more easily attained by self-employed people—entrepreneurs, professionals, and independent contractors, including millions of salespeople. I fell into this category when my children were small. In fact, an attraction of being a Mary Kay beauty consultant is the ability to earn a high income while working around the family's schedule. While some unenlightened corporations may tell their employees, "When you're on our payroll, leave your personal problems at home," Mary Kay Cosmetics has always had the philosophy that family has priority over career.

The other day, for instance, one of my secretaries had a look on her face as though she were a million miles away. I noticed her fiddling with some papers. "What's wrong, Nancy?" I asked.

"It's my father," she replied with watery eyes. "He's in intensive care."

She was obviously in no condition to be working that day, so I said, "Why don't you leave for the afternoon, Nancy, and be with your father."

"Oh, Mary Kay," she said, "thank you so much!"

I don't see how anyone could react differently in such a situation, but I'm told my response was atypical of corporate America.

I mentioned earlier that our salespeople can adjust their work around their family responsibilities. Women in sales positions at many other companies do the same thing, but what if you are in a nine-to-five job?

Joyce Grady knows that scenario. A Mary Kay national sales director in the Washington, D.C., area, Joyce formerly worked for the federal government as a full-time accountant.

"My children always came first," Joyce says. "However, if one of them got sick when a final report was due the next day, I didn't have a choice. No matter what, I had to get the report in. There were many, many times when I'd give my son an aspirin at night and pray to the Lord he'd be OK in the morning." These days, if one of her children is ill, she can just call another consultant to pinch-hit for her.

Flexible scheduling has great significance for Shirley Hutton, who became the first national sales director to earn over $7 million in commissions during her Mary Kay career. "When my children started school each year," she explains, "I would ask the principal for the master schedule for the upcoming nine months. Then I wrote every important event into my date book—football and basketball games, class plays, PTA meetings, teacher-parent days, everything. These were the days and evenings on which I'd know not to make a business commitment—times reserved for my children."

I know a thirty-five-year-old psychologist who does something similar. Her office is less than five minutes from her home, and she schedules appointments only from nine each morning to three in the afternoon—the period when her children are in elementary school. Another friend, an attorney, has arranged with her law firm to set her work hours around her children's school day. She knows the firm may not ask her to be a partner, but that is not her top priority. She figures when her children are grown, she will be able to work longer hours, and then perhaps aim at a partnership.

GETTING BOXED IN

Many women make the mistake of compartmentalizing their lives. They divide their priorities into separate "boxes." Faith is in one box, family is placed in another, and career is put in a third. Then they jump repeatedly from one box to another.

These boxes can be a source of frustration. In one box, a woman works for so many hours or days of the week, and then she moves over to her family box to be a mother, and then switches again to her career role.

Rena Tarbet, a national sales director in Fort Worth, Texas, says her work is not just a career but a way of life. She explains: "People frequently ask me, 'How many hours a week do you work in Mary Kay?'

"I might turn it around and reply, 'Well, let me ask you a question: How many hours a week are you a mother?' Then I'll ask her, 'How many hours a week are you a Christian?' I think of myself as a Christian and mother twenty-four hours every day, but this doesn't mean it's all I do. Likewise, I do Mary Kay around the clock, but this doesn't mean I just do Mary Kay. All of who I am and what I do falls together.

"During a typical day when my children were young," Rena continues, "I'd make breakfast for the entire family and get the kids off to school. After my husband went to work, I'd conduct a mid-morning skin care class. Later, I might meet a friend for lunch and do some grocery shopping. After school, I'd pick up the kids, drop one off at a piano lesson, and take the other over to the ball field. Around five, I'd pick them up, go home, fix dinner, and go out and have another skin care class or attend a meeting at my church. When I came home, I'd check the kids' homework and spend an hour or so with my husband before going to bed.

"So, when somebody asks, 'How much was Mary Kay?' or 'How much was family?' my answer is, 'Who cares?' Everything works together, and I never attempt to separate it into compartments."

To Rena, this is what having balance means. I agree. To me, this makes a lot of sense.

BURNOUT

I see it happen again and again. Women burn out because they can't handle all the things on their plate. In addition to their full-time careers and family responsibilities, they undertake social obligations, community activities, and an endless list of duties that are impossible to fulfill. With only so many hours in the day, they cut back on their sleep, and when they finally do get to bed, they have so much on their minds, they can't get a good night's rest.

Mickey Ivey, one of our national sales directors in Dallas, is a remarkable woman who always seems to be on top of things. Her husband, Charles, is a Southern Baptist minister who recently retired after serving a congregation of three thousand for many years; so you can imagine Mickey's active life. "Being a minister's wife is definitely a forty-hour-a-week job," Mickey says, "and particularly a Southern Baptist. An old Baptist joke goes, 'Not everyone can be the wife of a Southern Baptist minister—not everyone is physically able!'

"When my husband had his ministry, we had Sunday morning services, Sunday evening services, Wednesday evening services, and Thursday evening visitations; those were four weekly occasions when we were at church. Additionally, as a minister's wife, there were many luncheons and speaking engagements, plus I constantly taught classes. Most pastors' wives don't have careers because they have so many church-related responsibilities. But because my daughter and I both had more than our share of illnesses, our enormous medical expenses made it essential for me to supplement my husband's earnings.

"In our home, being a Christian was our highest priority. If Christianity is not evident in every facet of our lives, including our family life and career, then it's probably bogus Christianity, and that's not what God means for us to have.

"So we must have priorities," Mickey declares, "and if you've got them right—putting God first, your family second, and your career third—I truly believe you can adjust your fourth, fifth, sixth, and seventh priorities with no problem. But if you don't get those first three right, you're never going to do well in life."

Mickey Ivey is one of the busiest women I know, and despite having to battle some serious health problems, she's never shown signs of burnout. She attributes her focus and peace of mind to having her priorities straight.

Rena Tarbet says she also avoids burnout by maintaining balance in her life. During her twenty-seven-year Mary Kay career, this mother of three had a long-term bout with breast cancer that began in 1975. Rena underwent two mastectomies and reconstructive surgery, and later was diagnosed with cancer of the bone, which originated in the sternum. The disease also metastasized into her skull, left shoulder, and lower back. She underwent massive chemotherapy followed by cobalt treatments, and today, after more than a decade of fighting this horrid disease, she is in complete remission and has been for many years. Physicians familiar with Rena's medical history say it's a miracle she's alive.

During Rena's protracted health problems, she worked her career around her family and her illness, and made her Mary Kay business prosper. Becoming a national sales director with so many personal hurdles to overcome was a remarkable feat. When asked how she was able to manage, she says, "I believe you must have balance in your life; without it, you'll burn out. To live an ideal week, you have to set aside spiritual time, family time, career time, and personal time. Of course, it takes commitment to get it all in. But that commitment keeps you from giving in to temptations and pressures."

The number one complaint of career women with families and homes to manage is that there is never enough time to do everything. A woman with a nine-to-five job oftentimes will attempt to be Supermom and do all the wonderful things she believes she should do for her children. And thus, she tries to compensate by spending all her evenings and weekends with her children. Later, when they are asleep, she may feel guilty for neglecting her husband. As you can see, it can be a vicious cycle that can push her to the point of sheer exhaustion. She's always tired and, worse, stressed out. Not long afterward, she has burned out.

No matter how hard you try, it's often impossible to squeeze everything into your week. You have to pace yourself. Only by prioritizing can you achieve reasonable balance in your life.

OVERKILL

It's wonderful that today's woman has career opportunities that we only dreamed about when I was a young working mother. I look at young women entering medicine, law, and accounting, and I'm so proud.

But I want to give these women a word of caution. Even though you're working in a man's world, don't let your ambition detract from your womanhood. I've seen females become so aggressive in their climb up the corporate ladder, in their fervor to make law partner, or in their desire to be patted on the back by their sales manager, that they stop being ladies. In order to be accepted as "one of the guys," not only do they tolerate men using foul language in their presence, they lower their own standards. Soon, their zeal to be up there with the big boys changes them to such a degree, they may even lose the expression of their femininity by the way they dress. In their effort to imitate men, they compromise a major asset, their womanliness, and they are no longer good role models for their own daughters. Their aggression even carries over into family life. It begins to show up in their homes, and eventually, the subtle feminine touches essential to being a loving wife and mother are noticeably missing.

Here, too, you must have balance in your life. You can compete aggressively in a man's world while maintaining your femininity. Compromise in this area is unnecessary and will not be to your benefit. When men behave as less than gentlemen in your presence, you don't have to readjust your standards to theirs. Continuing to behave in a way that would make your mother proud establishes you as the standard-bearer. Let others elevate their behavior to keep up with yours. It may seem a prudish mode for the 1990s, but conducting yourself properly is timeless, and deep down, your colleagues know this. Men will respect you for being yourself, and it will bring out the best in them.

chapter 4

PLAN YOUR WORK AND WORK YOUR PLAN

*H*AVE YOU ever noticed that some people plan their vacations more carefully than they plan their lives? Before a trip, they read travel magazines and guidebooks, consult with travel agents, compare prices of different hotels and airlines, study routes on maps—all for a one-week holiday!

If only they approached their lives with the same consideration, imagine how much better those lives could be. Yet, a majority of people live from day to day, putting little thought into the future. Over the years, I have witnessed countless talented people who have no direction and, consequently, go nowhere with their lives. Other people with comparable talent go far and accomplish much—because they have direction.

No matter how much knowledge and ability you possess, you are doomed to experience minimal success if your efforts lack direction. Calvin Coolidge said, "Nothing is more common than unsuccessful men with talent . . . unrewarded genius is almost a proverb . . . the world is full of educated derelicts." I believe many people fail, not because they lack intelligence and skill, but simply because they did not concentrate their energy on a central goal.

Without a plan, your work will be in vain. This small difference in thinking has such influence on how our lives progress that we must give it high priority.

HAVING A PURPOSE

Did you ever get out of bed on a Saturday morning and have no agenda for the entire day? You had worked hard for five straight days and looked forward to a weekend of relaxation. So after catching up on your sleep, you got out of bed, washed up, threw on a robe, and fixed something to eat. Then you read the newspaper, made a few phone calls, watched some television, had lunch, watched some more television, had a snack, and took a nap. Before you knew it, it was time to fix dinner. Afterward, you went back to the TV, downed a late snack, and climbed into bed.

Think about how you felt after one of those days. In all likelihood, you felt groggy and down in the dumps. It's hard to identify why you were depressed, but you were. Actually, it's no wonder you felt lousy: you wasted a whole day! Twenty-four hours that you could never relive were gone.

Just as you drifted through an entire day without a plan and accomplished nothing, some people drift through their entire lives. They do it one day at a time, one week at a time, and one month at a time. The months run into years and span a life. It happens so gradually that they are unaware of how their lives are slipping by them until it's too late.

On the other hand, with direction you feel good about yourself. Think about the exuberance you feel after a long, hard day of work; even though you're dog-tired, you're excited because you have a sense of accomplishment.

Everyone needs a reason to get out of bed in the morning. The late John W. Galbreath, one of the United States' most successful real estate developers and a fellow Horatio Alger awardee, once told me, "I can't think of anything worse than going home at night without some concrete idea of what I am going to be doing tomorrow. I'd be lost. I wouldn't be able to sleep. Having a purpose is what keeps a person going." When Galbreath told me this, he was in his late seventies—an age when many people have long since retired.

People are happiest when they have goals, small and large, because they can look forward to attaining them. Think about it. Don't our biggest thrills in life come from realizing goals? In our careers, these may include making a certain number of sales in one month, earning a promotion, executing a major business deal, or building a large enterprise.

The same is true of what brings us the most happiness in our personal lives. Births, confirmations, graduations, weddings, and anniversaries are culminations of personal goals.

When we have nothing in our futures to anticipate, a void exists. Studies of terminal patients reveal that individuals who have future plans survive longer than those who don't. A cancer patient who is expected to live only three months, for example, may live six months to attend a son's college graduation or a granddaughter's wedding, and then pass away shortly afterward. It's amazing how often a dying person will hold on to life to experience a special event involving a loved one.

Having a purpose is so important to life that you must cherish your goal and give it priority. Of course, this means sharing it with your husband and children.

My definition of happiness is having something to do that you love to do, someone to love, and something to look forward to.

LONG-TERM THINKING

The race isn't necessarily to the swift; rather, it may be won by the long-term thinker. In most ventures, the long-term thinker holds a tremendous edge.

The world is rife with flashes in the pan—people who perform well for short periods but fizzle out over time. Among those who fall into this category are: the student who starts the semester staying up all night in order to ace each test but by midterm has fallen behind the class; the runner who leads the pack for the first quarter of the race but has faded behind the field by the three-quarter mark; and the salesperson who moves far ahead of the sales force at the beginning of the year but fails to meet his or her quota by the six-month point. Each of these strivers focused only on short-term gains.

A strong beginning is a good thing only when coupled with a strong finish. People may start out full of ambition yet never realize significant goals. Part of the problem is short-term thinking. Those who attend to the big picture are usually the winners in life.

By the time he was nine years old, my great-grandson, Jonathan Kerr, had won more than one hundred trophies (some six feet tall) for motorcycle riding. When I asked him, "Jonathan, to what do you attribute your success?"

He answered, "Grandmother, when the starting gun goes off, I get out in front, and I try never to let anyone get ahead of me."

The long-term thinking of the Japanese after World War II illustrates this point. Japan suffered perhaps more wartime devastation than any nation in the history of civilization. Throughout the 1950s, after more than a decade of rebuilding from rubble, the country remained weak. Yet a quarter of a century later, Japan emerged as an economic superpower.

The country's resurrection is one of the great economic miracles of modern times.

I read an interesting magazine article asserting that to understand this amazing recovery you must understand the Japanese culture. The article defined the Japanese word *mottainai* as "All things are precious, and to waste is a sin." We have no such word in our language, and until recently, we didn't need one. The United States has been blessed with so much. But we have transformed our vast land of plenty to serve a wasteful society.

Japan, on the other hand, has serious shortages of land and other natural resources. Over the centuries, this lack has caused its citizens to think differently. The country's 125 million people are crowded into a land the size of California, but the jagged mountains mean only 17 percent of the terrain is habitable. Japan's population density of 318 people per square kilometer is 3.5 times that of China and 15 times greater than that of the United States. Furthermore, Japan has practically no raw materials except water. The nation depends on other countries for more than 91 percent of its natural gas, more than 95 percent of its copper, 99.7 percent of its oil, and 100 percent of its aluminum, iron ore, and nickel.

With good cause, the Japanese culture behaves as though its survival depends on its ability to plan for the future. No wonder the Japanese government and Japanese industry spend impressive sums on energy research and development. In contrast, U.S. projects have been sharply cut back as the prices of imported oil fall. The Japanese government's policy gives research and development a long lead time rather than being influenced by any short-term abundance of low-cost energy.

The planting of bamboo illustrates the long-term thinking ingrained in Japanese culture. A bamboo farmer plants the shoot under the soil and covers it with clay, where it lies dormant for four years. Every morning, the farmer waters his

53

potential crop, and at the end of the fourth year, the shoot finally breaks through the ground. Then, in only ninety days, the bamboo grows sixty feet! Now during that four-year period, the farmer doesn't even know for sure whether the plant is alive. But he keeps the faith and doesn't abandon it. A long-term thinker must have this kind of conviction.

It's no wonder that Japan, a nation with relatively little land and resources, has made such tremendous economic strides. As Americans, we would be wise to study the Japanese culture and apply its valuable lessons in long-term thinking to our personal lives and careers.

QUARTERITIS

Many publicly owned U.S. corporations are afflicted with "quarteritis," a dread disease that can be fatal. This disease also affects us as individuals.

I don't know how it began, but publicly traded corporations in the United States today keep score of their performance on a quarterly basis. This means that every ninety days, a company's financial reports become public record. The information is available to any interested party, including competitors.

The actual purpose of these report cards is to make the investment community aware of short-term achievements by management. Wall Street keeps a scorecard because these interim reports affect the selling price of stock. Since a company has an obligation to serve its owners—the stockholders— management may be tempted to think only a few months ahead, so its traded stock will perform well. But a shortsighted company may make decisions that jeopardize its long-term objectives.

In 1968, Mary Kay Cosmetics was listed as a publicly traded company. In 1985, seventeen years later, our company made a decision to revert to private ownership. A major reason we are no longer listed on the New York Stock Exchange is because we determined that it was not in the best interests of our people and customers to make decisions based on short-term thinking.

It's interesting that the financial reports of publicly owned corporations in Japan are published only annually. The Japanese have little concern with short-term results. The shareholders in publicly owned Japanese companies are typically such business allies as insurance companies, banks, and other institutional investors who are aware that pressuring management to generate short-term results will hurt overall performances.

So the question is: Do you have quarteritis? There is a good lesson to be learned here. While short-term results are soothing, you must learn to think in terms of the big picture. Don't allow your desire for quick gratification to interfere with your long-term goals.

CONSTANCY TO PURPOSE

A favorite quote of mine comes from Benjamin Disraeli, the celebrated late nineteenth-century prime minister of Great Britain. He said: "The secret of success is constancy to purpose."

Surely most people start out with good intentions and want to make significant achievements. But too often they fall short of their ambitions because they lack discipline. They get sidetracked. People who work on their own—commissioned salespeople and the self-employed—without a supervisor to direct them are especially prone to this.

Because it takes true commitment to fulfill a long-term goal, Mary Kay Cosmetics has a "ladder of success," with the way to take each step clearly defined in black and white. Each person, through her own efforts, promotes herself.

A woman begins her climb by defining what she wants. Her next step is to visualize the completion of her goal. Then she must set a deadline. Once this is done, she breaks her goal into specific tasks and estimates how long each will take. She now knows what she must do each day to meet her objective.

I know many self-employed women who write down both their short-term and long-term goals, creating their own ladders of success. A successful life insurance agent told me, "When I first got my license, I decided on certain goals I wanted to accomplish, even writing down the dates I anticipated achieving each one. For example, I wrote down sales quotas: I planned to sell a million dollars my first year, two million my second year, and by my third year, I knew I'd hit the five-million-dollar mark. I figured out exactly what steps I needed to take to make the Million Dollar Round Table and estimated how long I thought each step would take.

"I set a date five years down the road when I would be a member of the National Association of Life Underwriters, and I knew I'd be a Chartered Life Underwriter by my sixth year." This woman had a purpose, and she didn't allow herself to get sidetracked. As a result, she accomplished all her goals and much more.

When I was living in Houston and had been working for Stanley Home Products for about three weeks, I attended a three-day sales convention in Dallas. At one meeting, a vice president delivered a speech that made a lasting impression on me. "Hitch your wagon to a star," he advised. Then he said, "Get a railroad track to run on." And, later, he said, "Tell somebody what you are going to do."

"What wonderful advice," I commented to a woman sitting next to me. Later that night, I read my notes and wondered how I could carry out his suggestions.

The following night at an awards banquet, I watched as a woman was crowned queen of sales for being the company's top salesperson. Along with the recognition, she received a beautiful alligator handbag. Right then and there, I decided that I would be the one stepping into the limelight the next year. By setting a specific goal to be queen of sales, I realized that I had hitched my wagon to a star.

"Now I need a railroad track to run on," I thought. Then it dawned on me that the queen of sales herself could provide me with my track. (In those days, Stanley did not have a written manual.) I approached the newly crowned queen and told her how wonderful I thought she was. Then I asked her to put on a Stanley product party for me. She consented, inviting me to her room later that night. I stayed for more than three hours. She did a sales demonstration and was kind enough to answer all my questions. The nineteen pages of notes I took during that visit became my sales presentation.

The following morning, I thought, "Now that I have a track, I must tell somebody what I plan to do." More than one thousand people were attending the convention, and I badly wanted to tell one of them. After looking around the entire room, my eye settled on the company's president, Frank Stanley Beveridge. I nervously headed toward him. After introducing myself, I said naively, "Mr. Beveridge, next year I am going to be the queen."

Had he known who I was, he probably would have laughed. After all, I had been with the company for three weeks and had an average of $7 per Stanley party. Fortunately, he didn't know that. Instead, what he saw was a determined woman who believed what she was saying. He gave my hand a gentle squeeze and, looking me straight in the eye, said, "You know, somehow I think you will."

I have no doubt he quickly forgot the incident, but that brief exchange had a profound impact on me because I had taken the third step. I had committed myself to another person—*the president of the company*. I couldn't let him down. I had to be queen of sales the following year. And I was!

Today, when a woman asks me how she can achieve her goal—perhaps to become a director or national sales director with our company—I think about my experience at that Stanley Home Products sales convention, and I offer pretty much the same advice I was given: Hitch your wagon to a star, find a railroad track to run on, and tell somebody what you intend to do. In addition, I emphasize the importance of writing that goal down on paper. "When you do this," I explain, "it becomes tangible." You can even write your goal on note cards that serve as constant reminders. Certainly you will be ever aware of your goal if you attach signs proclaiming your ambitions on places such as your bathroom mirror, the visor in your car, your refrigerator, and your desk.

Accompany your goal with a specific plan for accomplishing it. Break the grand long-term goal into a series of little goals, each attainable within a specific time frame. These little goals should be very reasonable, so you can simply go about accomplishing them one by one. As the saying goes, "A journey of a thousand miles must begin with a single step."

When our company was founded, one of my first goals was to conduct ten skin care classes a week. If I could do that, and then recruit other women to do it, too, I knew everything else would begin to fall into place. I broke that weekly goal down into two skin care classes a day, and at the end of each day, I crossed out my accomplishments one by one. At week's end, I got tremendous satisfaction from realizing my objectives, not to mention the money earned.

Have you noticed that when you thoroughly enjoy something, you can hardly wait to get out of bed in the morning to do it? One element you should add to my formula for attaining goals is to put enthusiasm into whatever you do! You're ahead of the game if you have found something you like doing so much you'd be willing to do it for free—yet it will pay you well. Your pleasure makes it easier to find the discipline and energy required to be a success. Your contagious enthusiasm will spread to your associates and your customers.

One situation that had bothered me about other companies was that no one told employees what they had to do to advance. People simply were supposed to work and wait until a supervisor said, "We have decided to make you a manager." When Mary Kay Cosmetics was founded, I decided that it would be easier for our salespeople if they had direction—if they understood what they needed to do to rise within the company. Hence, our consultant's guide spells out just what an individual must do to move up the ladder of success, making it easy for each consultant to set her goals. This was my approach in 1963, when we started our business, and today, each new Mary Kay beauty consultant receives this same advice.

WHY MOST GOALS ARE NEVER ATTAINED

The vast majority of people don't attain the goals they set, even when they know the formula I have just prescribed. Many only go through the motions, because they lack self-discipline.

They might get as far as defining what they'd like to achieve. They might even put their goals down on paper. And they may even briefly stick to a plan. But somewhere along the way, they slack off, and then it's only a matter of time before they shelve their goals altogether.

Shortly after I wrote my first book, a distinguished-looking businessman approached me at a fund-raising banquet. "Mary Kay," he said, "you could do me a big favor by giving me some direction on a manuscript that I've been writing for the past year or so." And before I could get a word in edgewise, he gave me a blow-by-blow description of his novel.

"It sounds great," I said. "I can't wait to see the movie!"

"Do you really like it?" he asked.

"You do a fine job describing it, but what do the people say who have read it?"

"I haven't let anybody see it."

"Well, what does your wife think about it?"

"Actually, she doesn't know I'm doing it," he replied.

"You've been writing a manuscript for more than a year and she doesn't know about it?" I asked in astonishment. "What's the big secret?"

"In case I don't get it finished," he answered, "I don't want her to laugh."

Then and there, I had serious doubts as to whether he would ever finish his book, let alone get it published. When I was writing my first book, every time somebody asked, "What's new?" I'd say, "Oh, I'm writing a book." Announcing my goal to my family, friends, and business associates put pressure on me to complete it. How mortifying it would have been to be asked a year or two later, "How's your book coming along, Mary Kay?" and for me to say, "I didn't finish it."

So when you have a specific goal, don't be shy about announcing it to the world. When people keep their goals a secret, it's usually because they don't believe strongly enough in themselves.

Once you have a long-term goal, you must establish a series of short-term goals to attain on a daily and weekly basis. For instance, a woman who opens a small restaurant may want to compete head-on with McDonald's someday, but she shouldn't start out focusing on running a ten-thousand-store operation. Instead, she should concern herself with operating her one restaurant successfully. She can set short-term goals such as increasing the quality of the food and the number of customers, with expansion as a future goal. Only when the restaurant is thriving should she begin to think about opening a second one. Then she must concentrate on how to make a success out of two restaurants without having to be present at both on an ongoing basis. After she works this out, she can expand her goal to owning a chain of restaurants and, later, adding to the chain. If she doesn't take it in steps, the persistent thought of becoming another McDonald's is not only unproductive, it's likely to overwhelm her. It's like the joke that asks: "How do you eat an elephant?" The answer is: "One bite at a time!"

As a small example of how you can tackle your goal, let me tell you about a rug I decided to hook for my foyer. I worked on it randomly, without much success. Finally, I decided that the only way I'd ever finish it was to block out a certain amount of time every day, and abide by that schedule. By measuring what I could reasonably produce in the space of one evening, I calculated that the rug would be completed on February 22 of the following year. So I began to hook the rug according to my schedule.

My first night's productivity was so insignificant that finishing the rug by my target date seemed an impossibility. Still, I knew from past experience that with daily persistence I'd eventually make progress. So each evening, I hooked my predetermined quota, and if for some reason I didn't fill my quota, I'd get up at five in the morning to finish the previous night's work. By staying on schedule, I not only made my target date, I finished the rug on February 21, one day ahead of schedule!

PROGRAMMING YOURSELF

The human mind is incredible. And, for that matter, so are the minds of all living creatures, large and small. God programmed a tiny spider, for instance, to weave a web. And if you have ever looked closely at a spiderweb, you know it's a complicated design. He programmed a salmon to swim thousands of miles upstream to the exact location where it was hatched.

One of my favorites of God's trillions of miracles is the swallows that arrive in San Juan Capistrano, California, on March 19. What's so amazing is that the swallows arrive every year on the same date—not one day early, not one day late—after flying six thousand miles across the ocean from Argentina. Then, every October, they make the return trip. For years, bird-watchers wondered how little birds that can't swim can fly such a long distance nonstop. Then they discovered that every time the swallows start their long flight, each one picks up a tiny twig to carry over the ocean. Now that's a heavy burden for a swallow! But the twig is quite necessary. Placing the twig on the surface of the water, where it floats, the swallow rests upon it. Following this break, each swallow picks up its twig and flies off again.

If the brains of spiders, salmon, and swallows can be programmed to perform such feats, imagine the capacity of a human brain. Our brain is sometimes compared to a computer. Using this analogy, the human brain is by far the most intricate computer on the face of the earth, far superior to any man-made computer.

As everybody knows, a computer must be properly programmed in order to operate at maximum capacity. We, too, must program ourselves to achieve our maximum potential. An individual does this by setting a long-term goal, writing it on paper, reading it repeatedly on reminder cards and signs, and imagining again and again the realization of the goal. Volumes of books have been written on the subject of programming our subconscious minds to direct us in reaching our goals.

In his self-help classic, *Psychocybernetics,* Dr. Maxwell Maltz writes that if you do the above programming exercise over and over, eventually a little voice in your subconscious will tell you, "Do that. It will help you get what you want." The same little voice also signals you, "Don't do that. It will be a hindrance to what you want." In time, according to Dr. Maltz, you will be on "automatic instrumentation," a stage in which the little voice steers all your actions in the right direction. Dr. Maltz's 1960 book states that either you can program yourself to succeed or you can program yourself to fail. It's up to you.

COORDINATING PRIORITIES

It's important to make certain your career goals are in sync with your priorities. Again, be sure you have your goals in writing, so you clearly understand what you want in life. But you need to have two lists, one with your personal goals and the other with your career goals, and they need to be coordinated with each other. People often fail to do this, and hence we see high achievers whose personal lives are failures. We all know of people who amass enormous wealth but can't seem to find happiness. As I said before, no matter how much money and how high a position a woman acquires, she will not know real success if she loses her family in the process.

Placing your family ahead of your career doesn't mean putting in so few hours that you neglect your work. After all, money may not guarantee happiness, but it does put food on the table and clothes on your children. If your family needs your paycheck to make ends meet, you can't shirk that responsibility.

But you may reach a certain point when you must weigh the accumulation of additional wealth against the added toil and time away from your family. I have a good friend who sells more than ten million dollars in residential real estate each year. Recently, this mother of three told me, "I had a shot at being my company's top residential salesperson. In fact, by early June, I was 15 percent ahead of the number two agent. But to keep up that pace meant working evenings and weekends during the summer—special times I usually block out to be with my husband and my teenagers. For years, we've taken six-week vacations in the mountains. Knowing how much my family enjoys these special times, my career had to be put on the back burner. I enjoy selling homes, but it doesn't compare to being with my family."

I congratulated her for having her priorities straight.

A woman with a chain of five cookie stores in a large Midwestern city told me a similar story. "A group of investors approached me wanting to put a lot of cash in my company," she said, "With some financial backing, they felt my local business could become a national franchisor with several hundred franchisees spread across the country. They said my business was the classic 'cookie cutter' and presented a wonderful franchising opportunity. It certainly was tempting. But after I calculated the traveling required, I declined. I make a very comfortable living now, and my family has no money problems. What's the point in building a giant cookie business that would demand longer hours, a lot of travel, and less time with my family? It is not my goal to be the richest person in the cemetery."

She, too, has the right priorities.

When husbands and wives both have active careers, it's crucial for them to be on the same wave length in their job-related goals. A friend of mine recently opened an art gallery. Her husband is a regional sales manager with a large Fortune 500 company and has aspirations to become a vice president. His promotion would entail transferring to the company's corporate headquarters in New York City. Unfortunately, this couple's career objectives are not in sync, because his transfer would mean she would have to uproot her gallery. No wonder she has confided to me that she is quietly ruing the day he has long been awaiting.

As a couple, you need to have a heart-to-heart talk about coordinating your careers with the home you buy, your children's schooling, your retirement, and so on. If you happen to be a successful working woman who has a professionally successful husband, I recommend that the two of you do what it takes to synchronize your long-term goals.

chapter 5

A MATTER OF TIME

SOME PEOPLE accomplish so much more in a day than others do. It's as if these high achievers had twice as much time at their disposal.

Over the years, I've observed that nearly all high achievers know how to make good use of those 1,440 minutes in each day. In contrast, other people seem to do things in slow motion. I think this is the type of person Groucho Marx was talking about when he said, "Either this man is dead or my watch has stopped."

I've always tried to manage my time. Some people may even think I border on being fanatical. I suppose this resulted from those years of being a single working mother with three small children. Back then, a day was never long enough to get everything done. Sometimes I felt as though I woke up in the morning already behind schedule. So out of necessity, I developed some good time-management habits. My survival and that of my children depended on it.

I used to clock how long it took me to do certain everyday things, and then I'd look for ways to do them in less time. I'd compete with myself against the clock on more efficient ways to put on my makeup, prepare meals, and clean the house. It carried over to finding quicker routes to and from work, avoiding rush-hour traffic, and shopping at the grocery store when the checkout lines were shorter.

Of course, I value my time as much now as I did then, and I'm still competing against the clock, trying to get the most out of my day. Once you get into the practice, it becomes a habit you can't seem to break. But then, who would want to?

In this chapter, I'll share my secrets on how to get the most mileage out of a day. I borrowed the majority of these time-management techniques from books I've read and people I've known. I applied them to what I do, refined them, and added a few ideas of my own. A word of caution: These time-savers require self-discipline.

THE "MOST IMPORTANT" LIST

Back around the turn of the century, Ivy Lee, a renowned efficiency expert, approached Charles Schwab, who at the time was president of Bethlehem Steel. Lee said, "I can increase your people's efficiency—and your sales—if you will allow me to spend just fifteen minutes with each of your executives."

"How much will it cost me?" the shrewd industrialist asked.

"Nothing," Lee replied, "unless it works. After three months, you can send me a check for whatever you feel it's worth to you."

"It's a deal," Schwab said, shaking Lee's hand.

The following day, Lee met with Schwab's top executives, spending only fifteen minutes with each in order to say, "I want you to promise me that for the next ninety days, before leaving your office at the end of the day, you will make a list of the six most important things you have to do the next day and number them in their order of importance."

"That's it?"

"That's it. Scratch off each item after finishing it, and go on to the next one on your list. If something doesn't get done, put it on the following day's list."

Each Bethlehem executive consented to follow Lee's instructions. Three months later, Schwab studied the results and was so pleased that he sent Lee a check for thirty-five thousand dollars. In an era when the average American worker was paid two dollars for a ten-hour day, this was a huge sum. Schwab was a man who appreciated value, and he figured Lee's advice to Bethlehem Steel was a bargain.

If Schwab, one of the smartest businessmen of his day, was willing to pay so much money for this advice, I decided I would follow it, too. Ever since, I've made up my own daily list of the six most important things I have to do.

Writing this daily list is one of the smartest things I ever learned to do. I believe in it, heart and soul. Each night, I put together my list for the following day. If I don't get something on my list accomplished, it goes on the next day's list. I put the hardest or most unappealing task at the top of the list. This way, I tackle the most difficult item first, and once it's out of the way, I feel my day is off to a good start.

Too often, people procrastinate, putting off the most difficult task until the following day—and then the day after that. You know what finally happens: that task gets shelved permanently.

The beauty of lists is they require you to write things down. As I explained in the previous chapter, when something is written down, it becomes tangible. If you trust everything to memory, you may never get around to doing even a well-thought-out task.

I value my six-most-important-things-to-do list so much it has been passed on to every Mary Kay beauty consultant. We even provide a "Six Most Important Things" notepad for our people. Those who use it improve their performance measurably. I'd be surprised if any of our national sales directors, the most successful women in our organization, are ever without a list during a typical workday. In fact, if they're like me, they probably keep a list on weekends and holidays, too.

Again, it's a matter of discipline. But once you work it into your routine, you'll wonder how you ever got along without it. Try it for ninety days, and see for yourself.

PARKINSON'S LAW

In 1958, Cyril Northcote Parkinson, the noted British professor and historian, authored *Parkinson's Law: The Pursuit of Progress*. It is the following single sentence for which the publisher and lecturer is most remembered: "Work expands so as to fill the time available for its completion." This is the famous "Parkinson's Law."

Long before I ever heard of Parkinson, I learned through personal experience the truth of his celebrated words.

Did you ever oversleep on a weekday morning? What did you do about it? You took a shower, put on your makeup, got dressed, and were out of the house in a fraction of the time it normally takes. By the same token, when you have all morning to get out of bed and start your day, that's how much time it takes—all morning! See? You're already familiar with how Parkinson's Law works.

This is why giving yourself a deadline is so important. I told you about my hooked rug and my daily quotas for finishing it. Well, I did it with Parkinson's Law in mind. Now take this book. I'd venture to say that the total number of unfinished manuscripts in this world greatly exceeds the total number of completed manuscripts. I know professional writers who write two to four manuscripts every year—and others who produce one manuscript every two to four years. A close friend of mine who writes full-time once told me he gives himself mandatory deadlines. Then, as I did with my hooked rug, he has a quota—a certain number of pages—to write each day.

"If a writer writes only two pages a day," he told me, "in six months, he'll have 360 pages—a full-size book."

I chuckled when he said, "Two pages a day is a piece of cake. I could do two pages every day before breakfast. On a good day, Mary Kay, I write as many as ten pages."

Again, it goes back to what Disraeli said about constancy to purpose—which reminds me of another of my favorite sayings: "If you want something done, ask a busy woman to do it." Isn't that the truth? That's because there are two types of people in this world: doers and those who do nothing. Busy people who appear to have more than they can do are the ones who come through when something important has to be done. Parkinson certainly knew what he was talking about.

TWO BIRDS WITH ONE STONE

One way to make the best use of your time is to double up—do two things at once. I will not be suggesting that you read a book while you drive to work. But doubling up is more than being able to chew gum and walk at the same time.

A long list of activities can be paired. For instance, while I put on my makeup in the morning, I listen to tapes. Most of these are motivational, but some are audio books that I haven't time to read. You can do the same thing while driving your car. Also I keep a small tape recorder with me, so that when I'm doing my makeup, driving, cooking, or watching TV, I can record intriguing thoughts that come to me. I've collected some of my best ideas this way. And we all know what happens if we don't get those thoughts on paper or tape immediately. We forget them. I have a writer friend who even keeps a small tape recorder under her pillow.

When properly used, a car phone is a wonderful time-saver. Obviously, it allows you to use your driving time productively for returning calls, making appointments, and so on. But keep two cautions in mind. First, limit the length of your conversations, because mobile telephone rates during business hours are considerably higher than rates for normal calls. Second, keep both hands on the wheel and your eyes on the road. You won't save any time if you have an accident!

Like most people, my patience runs thin when I have to sit in a doctor's reception area for an hour or so past my appointment time. But I've come to accept it as a fact of life, so I come prepared. I bring a large handbag filled with correspondence, magazines, and other work-related material, including my miniature tape recorder. I make good use of those waits. You can do this in all waiting areas, from train stations and airports to auto repair shops. Not only does it allow you to be productive, it makes the time pass more quickly.

DELEGATE

How many times have you said, "If there could only be two of me"?

The good news is there *can* be two of you—and more—when you delegate. When your time is worth dollars, don't do penny jobs. We follow this rule every day in business, but we sometimes forget to apply the same principle off the job. For in-stance, an executive who makes two hundred dollars an hour doesn't vacuum the office or type letters. He or she delegates.

A woman who owns a successful estate planning firm in Atlanta explained to me: "My time is worth a lot of money, which makes me high-priced labor. By delegating, I save money because things I would otherwise do are done by somebody earning less money. Of course, the most valuable use of my time is when I'm making sales presentations to a prospective client—something I can't delegate. But by delegating tasks such as accounting, bookkeeping, scheduling appointments, or making travel arrangements, I have more hours in the day to sell to and service my clients."

By the way, you can also have help who will launder and iron your clothes, shop for your groceries, and clean your house. In fact, depending on how much you earn, you can afford to pay somebody to do almost anything you don't like to do.

For example, many highly paid executives who work in New York City and live in such places as Greenwich, Connecticut, and Princeton, New Jersey, are driven to and from work by chauffeurs. Some would consider this extravagant, but to individuals who can be productive in the backseat of a limousine, the value of the extra work they get done during a two-hour commute far exceeds the cost of this transportation. On a larger scale, for the same reason, corporate jets exist. It's a matter of time and dollars.

BE PREPARED

The CEO of a large company once shared a pet peeve with me. "Mary Kay," she said, "I don't think there is anyone more presumptuous than someone who comes to a business meeting unprepared. When this happens, they waste not only my time, but theirs as well."

Yet, again and again, I see people fail to do their homework adequately, and these are people who should know better. For example, at a recent committee meeting for a local fund-raising group, the chairwoman apologized for not having read a seven-page memo that had been distributed to the committee members in advance. "Is there anyone else who needs to take ten minutes to read this material?" she asked sheepishly. Two people raised their hands, so for the next ten minutes, the six of us who were prepared had to wait while the three of them read the memo.

Later in the same meeting, the treasurer informed the group that a "personal problem" had prevented her from putting together some financial information the committee needed to make an important decision. Consequently, the committee had to meet again later in the week.

Many people in sales fail to prepare adequately. A real estate agent, for example, should always visit a listed property before showing it to a client. An advance walk-through allows her to anticipate questions in advance and have the right answers ready. The agent who does this is a true professional. All too often, however, a real estate agent will say: "I'm sorry, but I don't know what the real estate tax rate is in this area. I'll have to find out and get back to you," and "No, I don't know whether the bus stops on this block. I'll have to call you about that," and "I don't know what the house across the street sold for, but I could let you know if it's really important to you."

"If it's really important to you"! Why else would a customer ask?

I understand that it isn't possible for a salesperson to know everything ahead of time, so in many instances, I'll tolerate "I'll find out and get back to you." But when someone says this too often, he or she isn't properly prepared.

A salesperson can do all kinds of homework to prepare. For example, before calling on a large publicly owned corporation, you should at least read the annual report and some recent newspaper and magazine articles. This kind of information is available at stockbrokers' offices, libraries, and even from the company itself.

Proper preparation lets your customer know you respect his or her time because you don't have to ask questions to obtain information that was available for you to learn on your own. You also save the other person's time by being equipped to give prompt answers to his or her questions. Making the effort to be knowledgeable about a company signals the customer that you are conscientious and courteous, two qualities everyone admires.

From a standpoint of self-interest, being prepared is just good selling. In addition to the confidence it engenders, it prevents time delays that interfere with closing the sale.

PUNCTUALITY

In his bestseller *The IBM Way,* Buck Rodgers says he values meetings that are started on time, phone calls that are promptly returned, and memos that are answered when promised. I think he is on target when he refers to this as "calendar integrity," because it *is* a matter of integrity. As Rodgers states, when you keep people waiting, you show a lack of respect for their time.

I would go one step farther. When you arrive late for an appointment with your hairdresser, for example, you're actually stealing from her. While you wouldn't think of taking something that didn't belong to you, you stole her time. When someone gets paid by the hour, your tardiness takes money right out of his or her pocket.

I recently read an article about the owner of an expensive restaurant who, in small-claims court, sued a customer who had made a New Year's Eve reservation for a party of eight, didn't show up, and never called to cancel. The owner felt the reserved table could have been given to another customer, and asked to be reimbursed for the profit lost. Admittedly, the restaurateur took extreme action, but he had a valid case and certainly made a point.

When it comes to being on time, I'm one of those people who would rather arrive a few minutes early than risk being late.

Each July, a Mary Kay Cosmetics Seminar fills the entire Dallas Convention Center with approximately ten thousand of our beauty consultants. To accommodate everyone, four Seminars are conducted back-to-back. On the mornings of these spectacular events, at eight o'clock, each Seminar begins with the precision of a network television show. Ten minutes before eight, we begin a countdown. Above the stage, a large screen facing the audience reads: "Ten minutes till show time" and then "Nine minutes . . ." and so on until the final minute before the hour, when we start counting the seconds. At eight o'clock, Seminar begins. Now it's quite an accomplishment to get so many women up in the morning and have them all arrive on time, particularly if they've been traveling, are feeling fatigued, and need to be transported from hotels across the city. However, because everyone knows we start right at eight, we always open to a full house.

TIMELY TELEPHONE TIPS

I have an assortment of telephone tips to share, ranging from time-saving advice to simple courtesies. The first and best piece of advice I can offer is simple. You're probably talking too much on the telephone, so simply cut down your phone time.

During a typical telephone conversation, most people talk too much about too little. If you're making a business call, get down to business quickly. Chances are the other person is busy and isn't interested in small talk. Most businesspeople appreciate your getting right to the point. If you bombard someone with unnecessary calls, that person may even instruct his or her receptionist not to put your calls through. Build a reputation for valuing others' time by calling only when you have something important to discuss.

To avoid calls that eat up your time, you can screen incoming calls with an answering machine in your home or office. This permits you to take the necessary calls but avoid conversations with long-winded people who you know will talk nonstop for the next thirty minutes.

On the subject of answering machines, record a brief, clear message, such as: "Sorry to have missed your call. Please leave your name and number." Be sure the tone of your voice is friendly, so that your short message is not interpreted as abrupt or impolite. In addition, your message should not say, "Please leave your name and message, and I'll get right back to you," *unless* you intend to return every call promptly.

To get into the habit of keeping your conversations brief, keep a timer next to your phone. Awareness of passing time will compel you to shorten your telephone conferences.

Answer your phone in a "controlled rush." Invariably people will ask, "Did I catch you at a bad time?" You should reply, "I'm on my way out the door. How can I help you?" The controlled rush is a polite way of letting the other person know up front that your time is limited.

Receptionists should know to be courteous but firm when screening incoming calls. All callers should have to identify themselves so you don't end up talking to solicitors, survey-takers, fund-raisers, and others who might interrupt your workday.

As mentioned previously, Buck Rodgers's calendar integrity applies to returning telephone calls—promptly. I know one Fortune 500 CEO who makes sure all his calls are returned within twenty-four hours. If he can't make a call personally, he instructs his assistant to call for him. Even when he's traveling around the globe, this powerful executive returns the majority of his calls.

When properly used, the telephone is a wonderful tool for servicing customers. Sometimes a visit in person isn't necessary, but a telephone call will serve to remind your customer that you're thinking about him or her. And consider the time you save by making a five-minute telephone call rather than driving across town. Or, for that matter, consider the time and money required to make an out-of-town business trip versus a long-distance call.

On a final note about the telephone, for appointments scheduled weeks ahead, it's a good idea to get into the habit of calling a day or two in advance to confirm. Every salesperson knows the disappointment of a broken sales appointment.

SIXTEEN EXTRA TIME-SAVERS

In *It's About Time,* author Michael Shook points out that when based on an average life expectancy of seventy-two years, anything you do that takes twenty minutes a day will add up to a year over a lifetime. With this food for thought, the following list offers sixteen time-savers.

1. *Set your alarm clock for thirty minutes earlier than you normally do.* This adds two full days to your month! Place your alarm clock on the other side of the room, so you have to get out of bed to turn it off, and will become fully awake.

2. *Lay out your clothes before you go to sleep at night.* This keeps you from spending several groggy minutes in the morning wondering what you should wear.

3. *After you finish the dinner dishes, set the table for breakfast.* This saves valuable time during the morning rush.

4. *Know how much time to allot for routine tasks so you will be on time for appointments.* I know, for example, exactly how much time I spend from the time I get up in the morning until the time I'm ready to walk out the door. When you know how long you take to go through your morning routine, there is no excuse for being late to an early meeting.

5. *Allow extra time for the unexpected.* I give myself an extra ten minutes of driving time so traffic congestion won't make me late.

6. *Plan your meals ahead of time.* By knowing your dinner menu in advance, you need to make only one weekly trip to the supermarket. Some women make five trips a week! Once I had the pleasure of visiting Guam and meeting a beauty consultant there who was number one in her unit. She had ten children, and her husband demanded a hot meal on the table every day at noon. She conducted two

skin care classes each day, one in the morning and one in the afternoon. "How do you do it?" I asked her. Her secret was cooking each Saturday for the entire week. She made a lot of casseroles and soups—and made good use of her freezer. When she left home for her first class, she put a prepared casserole in the oven and set the timer for her return home.

7. *Don't waste excessive amounts of time watching TV.* Television has been described as "America's vast wasteland." If you're like most Americans, you're spending too much time visiting that wasteland. For example, on a weekly basis (according to *It's About Time*): Teenage girls spend an average of more than twenty-one hours watching television; women between the ages of eighteen and thirty-four watch an average of almost twenty-nine hours; women ages thirty-five to fifty-four watch an average of about thirty-two and a half hours; and women who are fifty-five and over watch about forty-one hours. Just imagine how much we could accomplish if we were more discriminating about which TV shows we watched. I highlight what I want to view in my *TV Guide* a week in advance. And I shut off the set as soon as any program I highlighted is over.

8. *Be properly organized.* Have a place for everything, and have everything in its place. By keeping things in the right spots, you conserve valuable time. In addition, what can be more frustrating than looking for an important memo that got lost on your cluttered desk, a blouse in a messy closet, or a cooking utensil in a disorganized kitchen?

9. *Organize your mail.* Handle each piece of mail only once. People generally read a letter, place it aside, and think, "I'll get around to it later," and they may repeat this process three or four times before they actually take action. Get in the habit of reading your mail only once. Usually the decision you make three or four days later is the same one you would have made when you first read the letter.

10. *Do laundry once a week.* Organize clothes according to colors, and do the washing on a weekly basis. Not only does this save time over doing it two or more times a week, but it can reduce your utility bills.

11. *Shop in advance for special occasions.* I have a large family that includes grandchildren and great-grandchildren, so I keep a "special occasions" book filled with data on each of them, including their ages. I buy all my birthday, anniversary, and Christmas cards at the same time each year, and when I shop for gifts, I buy them in quantity. Each January, I accumulate a closetful of presents for birthdays and Christmas. For the rest of the year, I never have to run out to shop, and I never miss somebody's special occasion because I was too busy to look for a gift.

12. *Set appointments at exact times.* When you make an appointment for 2:06 rather than 2:00, or 4:39 rather than 4:30, people tend to be punctual. Why? Because it gets their attention. They also remember the time better and sense that you mean business.

13. *Don't be a daydreamer.* A little daydreaming is pleasant, but many people spend too much of their lives daydreaming. Each of us has stared at a page in a book for several minutes without one idea

sinking in. When you begin to drift and realize you're reading at a snail's pace, put the book down and do something else until your concentration returns.

14. *Learn to say no.* Every busy person must learn to refuse some of the demands made on his or her time. If I accepted all the requests that come my way to serve on committees and boards, I'd spend every waking hour doing this. Although many committees are necessary, Milton Berle had a wonderful definition of *committee* as "a group of men who keep minutes and waste hours." Unfortunately, I have to say no to a lot of lunch invitations, dinner engagements, and other social functions. And as much as I'd like to participate in all of the good causes that request my time, there simply aren't enough hours in the day. Again, it's a matter of having priorities and commitments.

15. *Delegate.* Hiring a competent teenager to do your errands can save you several hours over the course of a week. This will also free you to spend more quality time with your family. Since so many teenagers are in need of extra spending money, finding a dependable helper is relatively easy.

16. *Let your children help.* Your children are a source of inexpensive labor. Let them assist you in such tasks as setting the table, preparing dinner, and attending to the lawn and garden. Not only do you save time, but your youngsters assume responsibility, which builds their character. This can also be an opportunity to do things as a family. And if you assign career-related tasks, it's good preparation for the future.

After talking with countless career women over the years, I am well aware that a major problem in their lives is finding enough time in the day. A young mother is challenged to squeeze in everything that she feels called upon to do for and with her children and husband. A single woman wonders how to uphold her commitment to her career and still have the time to enjoy an active social life. But in many ways, a single working mother has the most difficult situation. She must carve out enough time to nurture her children following exhausting days of providing for them financially. And, if she has a man in her life, her time with him translates into less time with the children. She experiences much conflict.

Whatever your situation, I hope my suggestions on time management in this chapter will help you fit more of the really important things into your day.

chapter 6

FOCUS

*F*OCUS CAN work for you or against you. You are either its master or its slave. A healthy focus helps you concentrate on your work, so outside distractions don't throw you off track. Focus provides direction, concentration, and intensity during your working hours by enabling you to block out anything in your personal life that is out of your immediate control.

On the other hand, when you leave the office, too much career focus detracts from your personal life. Such unhealthy focus causes you to lose sight of what really matters in your life—your loved ones.

As you can see, inappropriate focus can be dangerous. Finding the right intensity is the key. Again, you must have balance in your life.

HEALTHY FOCUS—WITH INTENSITY

While switching television channels, I happened to tune into a Dallas Cowboys game in progress. Although I am not a football fan, I found myself momentarily mesmerized by the announcer's description of the game: "The intensity of the Cowboys' defensive line is incredible! They're getting through the Broncos' front line as if they were playing a sandlot team. That twelve-yard sack makes it three in a row for the Cowboys. What intensity! What focus!"

I don't watch many football games, but I've heard enough broadcasters describe a team's intensity to know it wins games. And while I'm not a sports fan, I know that focused athletes are winning athletes.

Of course, having focus is necessary in our everyday lives, too. Have you ever noticed that some people come to the office each morning and fiddle around for several minutes before actually doing anything? These same people may go through the entire day without focus, producing, at best, a mediocre day's work.

Similarly, people who have focus zero in on their work the minute they walk through the door and don't let up until the last minute of the day. The rare individuals who perform at this level on an everyday basis are generally the best in their fields, whether engineering or brain surgery. With 1,093 patents, Thomas Edison, the most prolific American inventor of all time, called his ability to focus his greatest strength. Edison knew how to turn a liability into an asset. Though he grew increasingly deaf, he credited his hearing disability with enabling him to block out distractions.

In every occupation, focus is vital. A woman at work must be able to leave her personal problems at home. She should ignore distracting thoughts about the malfunctioning furnace, the poor report card her son brought home from school, and even the argument she had with her husband the night before. What she can't fix while she's at the office must be put on hold until it can be fixed. Like a fine athlete, she must focus with intensity so she can perform at her peak level.

CONVICTION

Focus is closely related to conviction. And believe me, it takes a lot of conviction to start a new business. This is especially true when you're surrounded by naysayers who are predicting your failure. Maintaining your convictions becomes even more difficult when well-meaning friends and relatives forecast your ruin. In my case, my accountant and my lawyer both warned me "for my own good" to abort my plans to go into business. It was hard to stand firm when they pleaded, "Mary Kay, don't throw away your life savings. You know nothing about the cosmetics business," and then went so far as to send me a pamphlet from Washington, D.C., stating how many cosmetics companies went out of business every day. My accountant said, "You can't give the kind of commissions you are proposing: you'll go bankrupt in six weeks." Had I listened to their advice, Mary Kay Cosmetics would never have opened its doors.

I imagine there are countless Mary Kay star performers who were warned not to join our company. One is National Sales Director Shirley Hutton, who, in the early 1970s, was a well-known television personality in Minneapolis enjoying a successful modeling career. She confided that her closest friends and coworkers tried to talk her out of working for a direct sales company. "In those days, a woman with a college degree didn't walk away from a television and modeling career to sell cosmetics," Shirley said, "and everybody I knew told me so." Just the same, she had the courage to go with her convictions—and proved the naysayers wrong!

In 1975, while her husband, Charles, was serving as an air force major, Pat Fortenberry, now a national sales director, signed a Mary Kay agreement. Pat couldn't wait to relay the good news. "I went running across the street to tell my best friend," Pat recalled. "But she looked at me with her nose up in the air, and said, 'Oh, Pat, I can't believe you're going to do anything like that!'

"Needless to say, I was discouraged, and I began to think, 'What have I gotten myself into?'

"Next, I called my mother in Mississippi. 'Mom, I am so excited. I started something new! I am going to be a professional beauty consultant for Mary Kay Cosmetics.'

" 'Four years of college, and you're going to peddle cosmetics?' my mother replied.

"If it wasn't for my husband, Charles, I would probably have given up right then and there. He told me, 'They are not the ones who have to do the work, honey; it's you. And if you've made a decision, you owe it to yourself to at least try.' "

Like Shirley, Pat went on to be a big success with our company because she was able to put aside the negative comments of others.

The Scottish essayist and historian Thomas Carlyle once said, "Every new opinion, at its starting, is precisely in a minority of one." When you have a new idea, the majority of people will resist it.

Imagine the conviction Alexander Graham Bell must have needed when he took his new invention to a bank to request financial backing. The irate banker told the young inventor, "Remove that toy from my office immediately!" To the banker, the world's first telephone was not a marketable product.

If you're thinking about starting your own business, remember that many great ideas were considered far-fetched and frivolous when they were introduced. Consider one of Great Britain's most esteemed scientists, Lord Kelvin, president of England's Royal Society from 1890 to 1895. Britons listened attentively when the lord made three predictions:

1. Radio has no future. 2. Heavier-than-air flying machines are impossible. 3. X rays are a hoax.

The philosopher Bertrand Russell was right on target when he said, "Even when the experts all agree, they may well be mistaken."

UNHEALTHY FOCUS—WITH INTENSITY

Like most things in life, too much career focus is not a good thing. Everything has its time and place, and when your time and place are with your family, you must be able to detach yourself from your work.

Oftentimes, a woman returning home at night brings her office with her. While she may go through the motions of having dinner with her family, her preoccupation with work means she pays little or no attention to what's going on in the lives of her children and husband. At the dinner table, the entire family can feel her intensity. They know where her thoughts are. After dinner, she's back to work, making telephone calls and going through a briefcase of papers. Weekends are pretty much the same.

For years, Mary Kay women have been told, "Work hard and play hard." When I say this, I explain the importance of being able to forget about your career during those precious times that are rightfully designated for your family. "Your family doesn't want to hear you talk shop all evening," I say. "Talk about their interests, not just yours. And on weekends, forget about your Mary Kay career. Don't even mention it!"

Kathy Helou, a Mary Kay national sales director and mother of two young children, is a good example of someone who works hard and knows how to turn it off when it's family time. "Because my office is in my home," Kathy explains, "my career is a part of our entire family's lives. For instance, I might be working at my desk when my young daughter, Jordan, comes in to ask me to fix her hair. I don't want her to think my work is more important than she is, so I take a break and do it for her. 'Mom, you're the best in the whole world at doing my hair,' Jordan tells me. A few minutes later, I'm back in my office, but throughout the entire day and evening, I'm going back and forth between my work and family.

"But it's important for there to be times when I'm totally away from my business—100 percent," Kathy continues. "To do this, when we're on vacations or just driving somewhere on a weekend, I'll announce to my husband and two children, 'OK, guys, today is not a Mary Kay day. Beginning right now, the first one who says the words *Mary Kay* is in big trouble!' At that point, the four of us are not allowed to mention anything to do with my work; whoever does may have to wash the dishes or do some other household task that night. What makes it so much fun is that the business is a big part of our lives, and we love it. So while this may sound like a silly game, it's actually very hard for us not to talk about my Mary Kay career."

Although my late husband, Mel, was very supportive of my career, he let me know that beginning at seven each evening, I was to be Mrs. Mel Ash—period. Starting then, it was *his* time. Mel knew how focused I was on my business, so I'm sure he felt that a rest from it was for my own good. In order not to disappoint him, I was always home by seven o'clock. No matter what I was doing at the office, I allowed myself the sixteen minutes it took to drive home so I wouldn't be late. I could be in the middle of a meeting, and I'd say, "Sorry, but I have to go." I knew that if I were late, I'd find Mel in a bad mood. Each evening, I knew I had sixteen minutes to change from executive to wife.

PUT ON A HAPPY FACE

Admittedly, focusing on your work is difficult when you have serious personal problems. For nearly a year after my divorce from my first husband, I felt as though I had failed as a woman. But with three small children to support, it didn't matter how I felt on the job; I had to be totally focused on my work, or my personal problems would compound! At the time, I was working for Stanley Home Products, making ten to twelve dollars for each sales demonstration; that meant doing three demonstrations a day to make ends meet.

So every day, I'd put on my happy face and act as though I were cheerful. When somebody asked, "How are you?" I'd answer, "Wonderful! And how are you?" Sometimes I said it through clenched teeth. I was certainly not going to tell them how I really was. Why tell them about my children's measles or the washing machine breaking down that morning? They didn't really want to know any of that, so there was no point in generating a negative conversation. Instead, I displayed enthusiasm, and this generated a positive reaction: I made a lot of sales, *and I became enthusiastic!*

After a seven-week bout with cancer, my husband, Mel, passed away at two o'clock in the afternoon on Monday, July 7, 1980. Two days later, on Wednesday, a Mary Kay conference was scheduled to take place in St. Louis. More than 7,500 directors and consultants were expected to attend. Many of these women had spent considerable amounts of money to be there, and I realized that if I didn't appear, I'd be letting them down. Knowing that the conference was supposed to be inspirational and that my mood was bound to affect them, I knew I had to put aside my personal feelings and put on a happy face. So, following the funeral, I packed my bags and headed for St. Louis. Even though I was grief-stricken, I did my best to project enthusiasm.

Great stage performers, especially those who work night after night in a Broadway show, have a wonderful ability to put aside their moods. No matter how sad an actress may feel inside, a role may require her to be jovial; she may need to laugh, sing, or dance. Or, when she is feeling happy, her role may demand that she express a melancholy mood.

Certainly you are going to have days when you don't feel like working. But these are the times when you must bring an especially keen focus to your work and not allow your lack of enthusiasm to deter you. A very successful man once told me, "Mary Kay, if I went to work only on the days I felt like it, I never would." I'm certain that if we all were candid, we'd confess to having bad days. Being enthusiastic is easy when everything is going your way, but the true test of your mettle is sustaining your enthusiasm during rough times. This is why I tell our consultants, "Fake it till you make it!" Or as Dale Carnegie said, "Act enthusiastic and you'll become enthusiastic."

FOCUSING ON PEOPLE

As a young woman, I once attended a sales conference where I waited in line for three hours just to shake hands with the vice president of sales. I was a brand-new salesperson for the company, and meeting him was important to me, so I patiently waited my turn behind several hundred others.

When I finally shook hands with him, he said hello, but he didn't even look at me. Instead, he was looking over my shoulder to see how many more people were still in line. He looked past me as if I were invisible. In my disappointment, I vowed, "If I'm ever in a position where people stand in line to shake my hand, I'm going to give each person my undivided attention, no matter how long the line is."

Now, people stand in line to shake my hand on many occasions, and I do my best to make every single person feel important. I try to say something personal to each individual, even if I don't know him or her. For instance, I might comment on a dress a woman is wearing or her pretty smile. I might tell an enthusiastic new consultant, "I'll bet by this time next year, you'll be a director." I can't tell you how many times I've made a brief remark like this, and sure enough, twelve months later, the consultant tells me, "Last year, do you remember what you said about how I would be a director by this time? Well, Mary Kay, you were right!"

There have been occasions when I had to shake hands with several thousand people. I'm often asked how I do this without becoming utterly exhausted. The answer is I keep in mind that each person in line has been waiting for as long as I have.

Also, when I meet someone, I give that person my undivided attention. While we talk, he or she is the most important person in the world to me. My eyes, my heart, and my thoughts focus on this individual. In addition, after I'm introduced to someone, I repeat the person's name. I do this for two reasons. First, it helps me to remember the name, and second, it's been said that the most pleasant sound to a person is his or her own name. Speaking the person's name whenever you're introduced to someone new is a good habit to develop.

Shortly after George Bush became President, I attended a reception in Washington. About two hundred people stood in line to meet the first family. When it was my turn to shake hands with them, Barbara Bush said, "Why, you're Mary Kay! I recognized you from your book. I really appreciated your sending me the book, and I enjoyed reading it."

The reception was a full six months after I had sent her a copy of my second book, *Mary Kay on People Management.* Right then and there, I knew she was going to make a great first lady.

I had the same kind of experience when I was introduced to Ronald Reagan during his presidency. He looked me squarely in the eye and asked me a few questions. Needless to say, it made me feel very good. I figure if the President of the United States has time to be this warm, shouldn't we all do the same?

A few years ago, a stockbroker who wanted me to open an account with his firm invited me to lunch at a popular restaurant. Throughout the meal, he kept looking around the room to see who else was there. He excused himself several times in order to table-hop, saying hello to influential business leaders. Perhaps he did this to show me that he was known by the movers and shakers of Dallas, but his inattention made a negative impression on me.

When somebody visits me in my office, my focus is entirely on that person. I don't like my desk to be a barrier, so I walk around it to sit in a conversation area with my guest. I usually have my receptionist hold my calls, but if I'm expecting an especially important call, I apologize in advance to let my visitor know there might be a brief, unavoidable interruption.

I wish store clerks would extend the same courtesy to their customers. I can never understand why a sales clerk will excuse herself to talk several minutes with a customer on the phone when there is a real, live customer in front of her. After all, a customer who takes the time to come to the store shouldn't have to take a backseat to a phone caller. I realize retail salespeople are instructed to be helpful on the telephone. Just the same, this clerk should say politely, "I'm sorry, but I'm with a customer at the moment. May I call you back in a few minutes?" Then she can resume giving the customer in the store her undivided attention.

MYOPIA

In 1960, Ted Levitt's classic article, "Marketing Myopia," appeared in the *Harvard Business Review*. Levitt wrote that business leaders should not restrict themselves to a specific industry. The buggy whip industry, for example, failed because its leaders confined their thinking to the manufacturing and distribution of horse-related products. They should have taken a broader view and realized they were in the transportation industry.

The railroad industry made the same mistake when it resisted the idea of manufacturing automobiles and building highways. The railroads tried to "derail" automakers, when they should have considered the horseless carriage an extension of the business they were in rather than a threat to it.

When television was introduced to the masses in the early 1950s, a decade or so passed before movie moguls realized they were in the entertainment industry, not just the motion picture industry. They learned not to limit themselves to making products that were seen only in theaters.

Each of us, in some way, suffers from myopia. Some of us become so focused on what we do for a living that we lose sight of the big picture. We may get so wrapped up in our work, we divert time and energy to our careers that really belong to our loved ones. As a result, our families—for whom we claim to work so hard—are neglected.

BIG ISN'T ALWAYS BEST

We live in a vast land, and our American heritage has long stressed size: big business, big houses, big cars, big boats, big buildings. Premium is even placed on big people. As a Texan, need I say more?

Our culture equates bigness with superiority. But, in truth, bigness is not always best. In many instances, a small prep school or small college can provide a better education than a much larger institution. The quality of life in a small community may be better than life in a large city.

On Wall Street, corporate success is measured by growth. It is not enough for a company to generate profits. If a company's revenues fall behind those of the previous year, the price of its stock often plummets. A publicly owned retailing business, for example, sells at a premium based on the opening of additional stores each year. If it fails to open a certain number of new outlets in a particular year, it loses favor with the investment community. But does having more stores make it a better company? Is the law firm with the most lawyers the best? Is the bestseller that sells the most copies the best book published? As you can see, contrary to what we have been conditioned to think, big is not always better.

So don't focus on building the biggest business. The end result could be lower value and poorer service to your customers. While it may generate tremendous sales volume, your big business's overhead may get out of hand, and even operate in the red. Your big ambitions may also result in less time with your family. Don't turn your focus away from what is truly important. Instead, learn to evaluate your success by the balance you achieve in your life.

chapter 7

DEALING WITH THE MALE EGO

I NEVER had any doubt that my late husband supported my career. Mel told me repeatedly that he was proud of my work, and I know he meant it from the bottom of his heart. Just the same, if I walked into the house a minute past seven any evening, it upset him, and he let me know it. I accepted his ground rules because his happiness was important to me.

By today's standards, Mel was of the old school. For the majority of his life, he lived in an era when a family had only one breadwinner, the husband. From Mel's perspective, the man had the responsibility to work every day to support the family, while his wife stayed home to do *her* work. Mel thought of himself as the strong male figure in the house and of me as the loving wife who saw to his dinner every night.

Mel was no different from most men in his age group. After all, these standard roles were established generations ago. When women became "liberated" in the 1960s, Mel's generation of men was so set in their ways, it wasn't easy for many of them to accept the rapid social change.

Even though you may not be old enough to have witnessed the social revolution of the 1960s, you can still feel its impact.

Like never before in the history of civilization, this movement brought change to the lives of women—and within a brief period. Any form of accelerated, extreme change, no matter how positive, requires time for large-scale acceptance. So three decades later, we still know of many husbands who balk at their wives having careers. And at six on a weekday evening, even men who claim to favor equal opportunity can be found casting longing glances at the bare dinner table.

Certainly, this does not apply to every husband. Some men have adapted well to the new woman. But a subtle resistance prevails among some men, even those who feel genuine respect for career women. It's a carryover from the old dictate that "a woman's place is in the home."

It will take a few more years before women's considerable progress is universally embraced. In the meantime, if you sense some resistance to your career from your husband, don't panic. Most likely, he is doing his best to adjust to the new woman you have become.

Perhaps the best way to influence a man's thinking is through verbal communication. Tell him that your career is as important to you as his career is to him. Whether or not he receives your feelings with unconditional approval right now, your careful explanations will help your husband to become more flexible in his thinking over time.

THREATENED HUSBANDS

According to a 1993 survey, in 29 percent of two-paycheck couples, American women earn more than their husbands. The same survey revealed that nearly 85 percent of female senior executives are responsible for over half of their household income. These figures reflect increasing numbers of women who work full-time, as well as falling wages for many men in the workplace.

Hundreds of Mary Kay directors make more than fifty thousand dollars a year, and many others make more than $100,000 a year. It is estimated that more women have earned over one million dollars from their Mary Kay careers than with any other company in the world. This indicates that a high percentage of our directors outearn their husbands. A casual observer, whether female or male, might say, "Now that's a problem I'd like to have!" But believe me, while it may seem amusing, it is sometimes exasperating. Some men can't deal with it, and some women resent their husbands for earning less than they do. A wife's large earnings can be a blessing or a bone of contention. Shortly, I'll share some ideas that have helped couples who find this situation troublesome.

With today's high cost of living, you would think any man would love for his wife to have a high-paying job—the higher the better. But this issue is emotional. Depending upon a man's age, his father, his father's father, and ancestral males from every past generation probably assumed the role of family breadwinner. If the wife worked outside the home at all, she had a part-time job to supplement the major family income. So while a clearheaded man should know his wife's capacity to earn a high income doesn't undermine his manliness, personal and cultural history may cloud his judgment.

A man who is secure about himself can find his wife's accomplishments a source of immense pride. Her success confirms that he made an astute choice of a lifetime mate. Her success is a credit to him.

Perhaps the real threat to a man's ego is not his wife's success but his own lack thereof. When a man who is struggling or even failing at his career sees his wife thriving in hers, he may think he is letting her down. Her success causes his expectations of achievement to rise, and failure to live up to those expectations deflates his ego. For this reason, a man may express his regret that he is not the one who makes the money. If he were honest with himself, he might instead say, "It's not that I have such a strong desire to be the main provider for the family but that I want to do better in my own career." Professionally successful men rarely feel threatened by their wives' success at work.

To add fuel to the fire, for generations many parents have encouraged their daughters to "marry well." In fact, an antiquated definition of a woman's success was largely based on her marrying a good provider. Consequently, when a woman earns considerably more than her husband, the thought may cross her mind that she has failed to marry a man who measures up to other people's definition of success. Even if this thought never surfaces in discussion, the couple may sense it. And bottled-up feelings can indeed stress a marriage.

WOMEN WHO SUCCEED IN CAREER AND MARRIAGE

Many women I know have achieved career success as well as happy marriages. But these situations don't just happen. The women worked to make them happen. Obviously, credit must go to the husbands, too.

Attitude has a powerful influence on how a man feels about himself. With the right attitude, his self-esteem remains intact no matter how much money his wife earns. Stella Sparks-Nowlin, a director who recently died of cancer, was married to a sheriff in a small Texas town. Although Stella started her Mary Kay career just to make a few dollars to supplement the family income, over time her annual earnings far exceeded his. Yet her husband understood that her success didn't reflect on his success as a sheriff. Texas sheriffs—even great ones—simply don't generate the high earnings that Stella could make with Mary Kay Cosmetics, and he had the self-assurance to accept that.

At a Seminar, a new consultant's husband asked Stella's husband, "Does it bother you that your wife makes more money than you do?"

Sheriff Nowlin answered, "As long as we're both playing a tune, I don't care who's got the fiddle."

Eddie Tarbet is also married to a national sales director whose earnings far exceed his. Even with a master's degree, Eddie, a social worker who works for an agency that places abandoned, abused, and neglected children into Christian homes, earns less than twenty thousand dollars a year, which doesn't match a good month's commissions for his wife, Rena. The belief that his work is meaningful keeps Eddie's self-esteem high. The Tarbets feel Eddie's work contributes so much to society that his level of pay does not determine the value of his occupation.

"Eddie is supportive of my career because he is secure about himself," Rena explains. "What he does for children is a wonderful contribution to this world. So when I'm put in the limelight, he doesn't resent it like some men would. In fact, the reverse is true: he thrives on it."

Still another man who appreciates his wife's career is Charles Fortenberry, a retired lieutenant colonel with the U.S. Air Force. "In his field, Charles liked the fact that a sales career offered so much flexibility, because I could work wherever we were transferred," Pat says. The air force moved the four-member Fortenberry family five times before Pat was named national sales director in 1984. Shortly thereafter, Charles retired.

"Charles liked the idea of having a business that we could share full-time after his military career ended," Pat says. If it were not for her husband's support, she asserts, she would never have made it. "In the military, the activities of an officer's wife revolve around her husband," Pat explains. "The air force expected a great deal from the wives. For instance, if a wife doesn't attend social functions, it's a black mark against her husband's career. So even though I wasn't employed by the military, just being an officer's wife in the United States Air Force was pretty much a full-time job by itself. There were many demands on my time, but Charles always backed me in my Mary Kay career. So many men talk a good game, but when it comes to actually giving the support and the freedom to their wives, they hold back. Never once did Charles say, 'What? You're going out again tonight?' or, when I was going on a business trip, 'Why do you have to go?' His support and encouragement made me feel I was always doing the right thing."

Charles was able to give Pat the freedom to grow in her career because, he explains, "In my own mind, I felt secure about what I had accomplished in my career. I did a good job and I was promoted for it, and I wanted Pat to enjoy that same feeling. I never felt I had to prove anything to other people."

From the beginning, the Fortenberrys had planned that, at his retirement, Charles would join Pat in her business. Now he supports her by doing administrative work and handling their taxes and investments.

John Harris, whose wife, Jan, is a Mary Kay national sales director, also gets questions about his attitude toward her earnings. John says, "The way I look at it is that when we were first married, I worked two jobs and Jan was home.

Everything went into the same checking account, and later, when we both worked, it still went into the same pot. To us, our marriage is a fifty-fifty deal. What's mine is yours, and what's yours is mine. We both have the same goals for our family, so it doesn't really matter who contributes what or when, does it?"

It takes a special husband to give his wife's career unconditional support. A man who is comfortable with himself doesn't feel threatened by his wife's success. It also takes a special type of woman to realize that her husband's masculinity is not measured by his earnings. This, too, requires self-esteem.

MONEY MATTERS:
YOURS, MINE, AND OURS

Many two-income families keep two checking accounts—a departure from the days when families typically had one income and one joint checking account. Then, the husband brought home the sole paycheck and, consequently, had nearly absolute control of the finances. As recently as the 1950s, it was common for the husband to write all the checks.

Today's female work force is involved in family finance. Not only do women share in decisions about where money is spent, they spend considerable amounts on their own. A wife doesn't have to consult her husband when she makes a purchase, whether it's a new outfit or a new car. Alternatives to the traditional family budgets of our parents have ended a woman's need to seek permission from her husband to spend her own hard-earned money.

A family's earnings can be divvied up in several ways. There is the old-fashioned method, where it all goes into a common pot, and what's mine is yours and vice versa. This approach has pros and cons. On the plus side, you operate as a team. On the minus side, you and your husband could clash on everything from mathematical errors in the checkbook to how much to spend on what.

Of course, with separate checking accounts, disputes may arise over *who* pays for what; in other words, does it come out of your funds or out of his? Some friends of mine solve this by having three checking accounts: yours, mine, and ours. The "ours" checking account is a common fund for joint purchases, savings, and investments. Major expenses such as mortgage payments, home improvements, insurance, and taxes are paid from the common account.

When I am asked whether I approve of prenuptial agreements, I say it depends on the circumstances. For young couples just starting out, when neither one has any assets, I'm against prenuptial agreements. Newly married people who were divorced or widowed earlier in their lives have entirely different needs. A prenuptial agreement can be useful when there are grown children from previous marriages. A wealthy widow, for instance, might want to ensure that her assets are inherited by her own children, rather than by her second husband or his children.

A MATTER OF TEAMWORK

The concept of teamwork has generated much talk in the workplace. But teamwork in marriage has always been in vogue. It's essential to a successful marriage, but the concept has undergone some changes.

In past generations, the roles within the married team were straightforward. The man was to work every day in order to support the family financially. His wife was to attend to a variety of household tasks, ranging from cooking to child care. One thing was clear: the wife's responsibility was the home. She did whatever was required to fulfill this responsibility, whether her husband worked long or short hours. No matter how many family members lived in the house or how many hours it took to get everything done each week, she had a job to do, and she nearly always did it with little or no help from her husband.

From the days when the female stayed in the cave while her mate went out to hunt for food until the second half of this century, the roles of husband and wife remained essentially the same. But in the 1960s, women began entering the American work force in huge numbers, forever altering the teamwork arrangement between husband and wife. Suddenly millions of women were working as many hours at their wage-earning jobs as their husbands were, and these women found they could no longer carry the entire load of household tasks. They began to insist that the husbands share the load.

Attitudes about household tasks have changed. When a man's wife is generating a healthy second income, he can no longer expect her to do all the housework during those precious few hours she has to spend with her family. As a result, the responsibilities of husbands and wives are being redefined in families across America. The woman is no longer the sole diaper-changer or the only one to help the children with their homework. These days, more and more husbands can be found in the kitchen and in the laundry room.

As a sign of the times, Jan Harris likes to tell the story of her son, Jake, then seven years old, who approached his father in the kitchen late one afternoon. "Say, Dad," Jake asked his father, "would you teach me how to cook?"

"Why, sure," John answered.

"Great, Dad. It's something I'll need to know in case I ever marry a Mary Kay director."

Across America, millions of little boys like Jake Harris are learning from their fathers how to be good husbands.

What's more, today's young career woman probably has an understanding with her husband. Chances are, if they were both working full-time during their courtship, they discussed sharing the household tasks before they got married. *Before* wedding vows are exchanged is the best time to negotiate the arrangement, spelling out who will do what when they begin keeping house. Although ground rules should be established, the arrangement needn't be cast in stone; it may require re-negotiation if the work turns out to be unfairly divided. With an understanding from the beginning that they maintain throughout their marriage, husband and wife can work as co-captains of an efficient, satisfying team.

chapter 8

SPECIAL TIMES

I DON'T think anybody ever said from their deathbed, "I should have spent more time at the office!"

When you look back at the good times you had, it won't matter how much money you made, how much overtime you put in, or how many evenings and weekends you worked at home to catch up on what you didn't get done at the office. Instead, you're going to think about all the precious moments you spent with your loved ones—special times that had nothing to do with your work.

Too often, people forget that the reason they work so hard is to provide their families with the finer things in life—which includes leisure time with them. Hard work is only the means to an end.

The older you get, the more you realize that life goes by quickly, and that those who don't stop to smell the roses truly miss out. While your children are small, take the time to do things with them, because they grow up all too soon!

The modern problems of youth—dropping out of school, teenage pregnancy, drug use, criminal activity—can usually be traced to a lack of quality parental time. With these serious issues in the headlines, make sure your own children don't become delinquent because you weren't around to guide them.

WORKING YOUR CAREER
AROUND YOUR CHILDREN

You recall that some Mary Kay mothers look at their children's school calendars each fall and note important dates, ranging from football games to school plays, so they can plan their work around their children's activities. Of course, not all careers offer this degree of flexibility; quite often a working mother has no choice but to do the opposite: plan time with her children around her job.

It's unfortunate to be placed in this position. Our company is experiencing tremendous growth because the women who work with us can allow time for their husbands and children first, working around their needs.

Naturally, a working mother with this flexibility must be careful not to overuse it. When earnings are based upon sales, as with our people, there's a definite correlation between hours worked and money made. In other words, go ahead and schedule time off to watch your daughter play in a softball game or attend your son's piano recital. But you should then make up for the work you missed.

Depending on your job, flexibility may also be possible when you're on salary. There may be many variables to play with; it's up to you to come up with creative ways to work your job around your family.

Some lines of work offer little or no flexibility. Fortunately, enlightened business leaders make some options available to their employees. Explore whatever options may be worked out with your employer. And if you're in the market for a new job, look for a company that is sensitive to family needs. During interviews, don't be shy about asking direct questions regarding management's policies on such issues. Knowing where a prospective employer stands on these matters can help you make a decision that will lead to career satisfaction.

WORKING YOUR CAREER AROUND YOUR HUSBAND'S CAREER

Depending on your husband's occupation, you may have to arrange your career around his. Women married to corporate executives know this necessity. I read that Robert Beck, former CEO of Prudential Insurance Company of America, was transferred fourteen times during his first twenty years with the company. The former CEO of United Airlines, Richard Ferris, moved ten times in ten years as he worked his way up the corporate ladder. Of course, top executives aren't the only ones who have to move frequently. Military personnel, coaches, and many others experience the same thing.

When a family man's employer relocates him, it not only uproots the family, it usually means his wife will have to adjust her career to their new locale. It would be ideal if your husband's company moved you to a city where you could find a position just like your previous one, but since the odds are against this, what you need is a career so flexible that you can work anywhere.

It is also becoming common for women to be transferred to other cities, requiring husbands to relocate their careers. Today, the decision of whose career adjusts to whose often comes down to economics. Obviously, if a wife's income or job potential is greater than her husband's, they must consider this a significant factor in evaluating a decision to relocate.

While the ability to relocate with ease is an attractive feature of a Mary Kay career, it is not exclusive to our sales force.

Other careers provide similar flexibility. A woman in tele-marketing doesn't need to feel tied to any one place. A stock-broker doesn't have to live in Atlanta to service clients in Atlanta. And a woman operating a business out of her home can likely take her business to her new home in another city.

Rosanne Rosen, a free-lance writer and the author of *Marriage Secrets: How to Have a Lifetime Love Affair,* says she carefully chose a career that would not conflict with the demands of her husband's business but would still be fulfilling to her. "Once our two daughters were in high school," Rosanne explains, "I wanted to work full-time, but I didn't want to get bogged down in a nine-to-five job on a newspaper. Mark owns a successful spirits and wine marketing company, and with the girls gone, I frequently accompany him on business trips. Well, no employer would put up with my traveling a dozen or so times every year. . . . I knew my work had to provide me with the freedom to pick up and go at any time—without asking a boss for permission. From an early age I had fantasized about living the life of an author, and knowing I needed a career with flexibility, I decided to pursue my dream by trying my hand at writing books. As a writer, I have been able to maintain just the right balance between my marriage and my career. I spend lots of time with my husband, and my work is portable, so I can take it with me when we travel."

As it turned out, Rosanne's need to coordinate her career with her husband's career is helping her dream come true. Of course, not everyone can write for a living, but I know women with sales positions in such fields as insurance and real estate who also enjoy this flexibility. Other friends of mine work on a limited basis in legal and accounting profes-sions. Sometimes this flexibility means sacrificing peak earn-ings, but what matters is that a woman is happy and fulfilled by her work.

GETTING YOUR CHILDREN INVOLVED IN YOUR WORK

I recently read an article about a leading Broadway actress who has two children in elementary school. Because this young mother performs in plays in the evenings as well as weekend matinees, she was unable to spend as much time at home with her children as she wished to. So what did she do? Before accepting a role in an ongoing production, she took her husband and two children to see the departing actress perform in the play. Her family could then participate in making the decision with her. Their involvement made them supportive, and the three of them voted for her to take the part. (Remember: People will support that which they help to create.) Once a week, one of the children accompanied her to the theater to watch the play backstage. Not only did this permit the mother to spend time with them, they had memorable experiences that few children ever go through.

My son Richard has often said that he was born in direct sales. "I started helping to fill orders for my mother when I was three years old," he told a packed auditorium at the Dallas Convention Center.

Richard was indeed only three when he and his older brother and sister, Ben and Marylyn, spent every Saturday morning helping me fill my orders for the week. We had to sort the entire week's supply of merchandise I had sold, so the four of us would have everything spread all over the garage of our small home. Every item had to be packed, and while the boys organized what belonged in each order, Marylyn did the paperwork, checking off each piece of inventory before it went out the door. We usually finished by noon. With one of the children accompanying me, it took the rest of the day to deliver everything to my customers' homes. This crash course in business was a way for us to spend time together—time that my work would otherwise have taken from my children.

Many Mary Kay consultants get their children involved in their careers the same way. Most kids are looking for a part-time job to earn extra spending money. One advantage of running a business from your home is you'll find lots of odd jobs to give your children. When you have confidence in them, you'll be surprised how well they can perform tasks you might have thought were over their heads. For example, today's youth are much more comfortable with computers than previous generations. And what they don't already know about computers, they seem to learn quickly. So perhaps one of your children can help to update your records on the computer.

Exposing your children to your work lets them pick up people skills that other children don't have opportunities to learn. A good example is the eleven-year-old daughter of one of our top sales directors, Lisa Madson. "I couldn't help eavesdropping on Rachel when she picked up the downstairs phone and carried on a very grown-up conversation with one of my out-of-state consultants," Lisa says. "Neither of them was aware I had picked up the upstairs phone, and the new consultant was excited to tell somebody about having recruited her first woman into the business. Never having met Rachel, the consultant evidently thought she was talking to an older child when she said, 'I called to let your mother know I have a new business associate.'

" 'Really?' Rachel asked with enthusiasm. 'Well, good for you! Congratulations!'

"I was beaming with pride," Lisa continues. "She repeated practically word for word what I would have said. I had said the same thing many times, and Rachel had picked it up. She understood that it was important for the woman to share her excitement with somebody, and since she didn't think I was home, she pinch-hit for me."

Joyce Grady, a national sales director, tells a story about her son. Early in Joyce's career, she set a goal to earn the use of a new car. "When I fell short of my goal, I was so disappointed. I thought I had qualified for the car, but found out I had missed by a narrow margin," she says. "So later that day when my son walked into the house after school, there I was sitting on the sofa, down in the dumps.

"Seeing the sad expression on my face, he asked, 'What's wrong?'

" 'Oh, honey,' I said, 'I didn't get the car.'

"He patted me on the back and said, 'It's OK, Mom. You can do it. You can make it next month!'

"He cheered me up immediately. I was especially proud of him because I knew exactly where his pep talk had come from. He had heard me say to many of my consultants, 'You can do it. You'll do it next month!' "

Many young children have learned to listen intently and praise people because they've seen and heard their mothers doing it. What wonderful exposure they're getting! Imagine how these skills will benefit them with their school friends, teachers, and others they encounter.

Depending upon your occupation, you can delegate various tasks to your children. If you work in an office, take them to work with you during a school holiday as a special treat (after clearing this with your supervisor). They will treasure the memory of this wonderful experience later in life.

ONE-ON-ONE TIME

A common complaint expressed by children and husbands of career women is: "She's too busy for me." Many times, what they really mean is: "I don't get enough time alone with her."

On the other hand, the common complaint of working mothers is: "There is never any spare time." The consequence is constant tension; these mothers are always trying to squeeze more into each working day. A typical lament is: "I wanted to help my son on his science fair project, but I have a business meeting tonight."

Working forty or more hours a week doesn't permit much quality time with loved ones. Some women manage better than others, depending on how much their husbands and children pitch in or whether they can afford hired help.

After coming home from the office and completing their household tasks, most working mothers use up their last ounce of energy participating in group activities with their families. From going out to dinner to taking in a movie as a family, it's called "togetherness." Simple arithmetic dictates that everything is done as a group: after subtracting the hours necessary for work, there aren't enough hours left in the day to spend individual time with each member of the family. Nevertheless, try to figure out a way to spend one-on-one time with each of your loved ones so they don't feel shortchanged. Your husband and your children need some time with you as individuals.

Let's first talk about your husband. Obviously, by simply sharing a bedroom with you, he does get some private time. But this alone is not sufficient. To add the spice of romance to your marriage, make "dates" with him. A date may be a late dinner for two after the children have eaten, a walk at dusk, or dessert at a quiet restaurant. And while family vacations are wonderful, get in the habit of occasionally traveling with just your husband. A one-week holiday or several weekend trips each year can get you away by yourselves for a much-needed feeling of renewal.

Each of your children also needs one-on-one time with you. When my children were young, I always found some time to spend with them individually. Often I had no choice but to kill two birds with one stone by getting them involved in my work. During errands or on our Saturday afternoon trips to deliver orders, we'd have serious talks.

In addition, we observed "Richard's Day," "Ben's Day," and "Marylyn's Day." For instance, on Marylyn's day, she and I would take in lunch, and spend the afternoon looking at clothes for her. In her adult years, the two of us continued to go on shopping sprees together, to recapture the good times we shared.

When your children are older, they will cherish these one-on-one times. One national sales director, Jan Harris, remembers that when her children were small, each would have a "goof-off day" to spend with her. On these special occasions, the child could choose what he or she wanted to do with Jan, whether a movie, a visit to the zoo, or a trip to the amusement park. Prior to her daughter's wedding, Jan was cleaning out her daughter's closet when she came across a box filled with mementos of her childhood. Inside was a note she had written as a fifth-grader to her mother: "Dear Mom, I am ready for a goof-off day. Can we have a goof-off day on Friday?"

Unlike their big sister, when my sons were little, they weren't into shopping with their mom. Often I spent Ben's Day and Richard's Day watching them play baseball. I was continually looking for new one-on-one activities that my boys would enjoy. As a woman, it was a real challenge to do the kinds of things that a father would have done with them. I confess I had to work at coming up with creative ideas.

Mary Kay moms tell me there are many more choices today, particularly for a mother who can schedule her work around her children. One mother tells me she picks her daughter up at school twice a week to have lunch at a local fast-food restaurant. Another mother plays tennis with her son, and still another spends one-on-one time with her daughter on the golf course. It seems that mothers are finding interesting things to do with their children, from taking music or art lessons together to going on exotic vacations. As our society becomes more affluent, additional options become available.

In addition, recreational activities are abundant today. Most areas have theme parks and petting zoos (which didn't exist when my children were small). Reduced weekend airfares and family packages being offered by hotels make it easier for a working mother to get away with her husband or even with one of her children.

ONE-ON-ONE GAMES

In 1978, Lane Nemeth founded Discovery Toys, in part because she wanted parents to interact more with their children through playing games. "A prime purpose of our games," Lane explains, "is to get kids and their parents away from the television set and video games, so they can interact with other human beings. This way, they develop valuable social skills. When a parent and child play a game, it's a wonderful way for them to communicate with each other. You'd be surprised how much conversation comes from a game board that wouldn't surface at the dinner table."

A product cannot become part of the Discovery Toys line unless there is more than one way to play with it; the toy must exercise a child's imagination. In addition, the toy must have a purpose in the child's development, whether educational, creative, physical, or all three. And naturally, the toy has to be fun.

Long before Discovery Toys existed, I shopped for the kind of toy Lane Nemeth's company sells. When my children were small, I looked for educational books they would enjoy having me read to them. In particular, I chose bedtime stories that were not only interesting but also taught a good lesson or moral. Reading bedtime stories is a wonderful way to spend quality one-on-one time with a small child. It has a calming effect on both mother and child, and this makes a story, along with a prayer, a very special way for a little boy or girl to end the day.

Reading to children also develops an interest in books at an early age, which can result in a lifelong habit of reading. What an enjoyable and educational gift you can bestow!

JUST FOR YOU

A woman who neglects herself is not an asset either to her work or to her family. Even so, many women who strive to be good wives, mothers, and workers forget—or don't have time—to take proper care of themselves. The stress women experience fulfilling these roles may not only take the joy out of their lives, it could also prove harmful to their health.

Again, remember your priorities. The purpose of work is to provide happiness and security for your loved ones *and* for you. Your happiness and theirs are intertwined; what's good for you is ultimately good for them, too. To a large degree, the mother sets the mood for the entire family. When she appears satisfied and cheerful, her husband and children will likely emulate her attitude; unfortunately, her negative moods also are contagious.

When your husband or children are sick, you are the one who takes care of them. But what will happen if you become ill? Who will take care you? To stay healthy, you must eat nutritious foods, exercise, and pursue activities that reduce stress in your life. So maintaining your health could very well mean more relaxation and even, on occasion, pampering yourself.

I must confess that when my children were young, I didn't indulge in certain luxuries that probably would have been good for me. At night, after I did what had to be done for the family, I could only fall into bed. In retrospect, perhaps I should have "found" the time. But back then, a working mother felt guilty enough just for having a full-time job!

Some of the successful women at Mary Kay Cosmetics have made the following eight "just for you" recommendations:

1. Take a hot bubble bath at the end of the day to unwind.
2. Treat yourself to a good professional massage.
3. Every now and then, when your batteries need recharging, go to a spa for a couple of days.
4. Spend quiet time by yourself with a good book.
5. Get into the practice of regular exercise. Consider swimming, aerobics, or just walking.
6. Spend some time with only your girlfriends. It's healthy to have women friends.
7. Take a weekend to visit a college girlfriend in another city.
8. Take good care of your skin and use quality cosmetics to make yourself look and feel beautiful. Your entire family will benefit from how this affects you.

Incidentally, I would have added this last recommendation even if I weren't in the cosmetics industry. You see, I truly believe in what we sell!

chapter 9

TAKING YOUR
BUSINESS SKILLS HOME

$\mathcal{A}$S A working mother, you can take home abilities that you learn at the office. The people skills that carry you through the day with your coworkers and customers will also go a long way with your husband and children. You can apply your time-management proficiency to budgeting your family schedule and running your household.

I bring this to your attention because people sometimes forget to use the same tools at home that contribute to success at work. This chapter covers a variety of transferable work-related virtues—everything from being a good listener to praising others. Moreover, you can pass these skills on to your children. We enhance our children's lives by serving as good examples through our behavior. It is not a good idea to advise our children, "Do as I say, not as I do." You probably resisted this advice when you were young, and your children are likely to do the same.

Of course, we can't run our homes like businesses. Retired military officers and former corporate executives may try to rule their homes with the same rigid discipline they applied to their subordinates at work, but this approach represses the love and warmth that a family needs. We must be nurturing; there is no place—in either a business or a family—for a dictator.

THE ART OF LISTENING

Every credible people-management book written during the past decade has devoted at least a few pages to the importance of being a good listener. The advice usually stresses the importance of listening to your people, and letting them know you respect their opinions.

In business, managers are taught to listen, because workers feel appreciated when they know their supervisors hear them. This good feeling motivates the workers, who then perform better at their jobs.

The same principle applies to how salespeople treat customers. Good sales managers stress that to understand customers' needs, listening to them is crucial. Salespeople are told again and again, "God gave you two ears and only one mouth because He meant for you to listen twice as much as you speak." Being a good listener is a prerequisite to being a successful salesperson.

No matter what you do in the world of business, you must have sharp listening skills. If you're currently enjoying a successful career, you probably already listen well to your coworkers and customers. But are you listening when you come home from the office? Are you so preoccupied with your job that you shut out or minimize what your husband and children have to say? Many career mothers fail to apply at home what they've learned at work.

Your family deserves the same respect you've been trained to give your coworkers and customers. Place a high value on recognizing their needs. Failure to listen carefully has the same adverse effect on household morale that it has in the office.

Listen to each member of your family as if he or she were the CEO of your company or your most important customer. I know you wouldn't sort your mail while your boss was in your office. Nor would you read the newspaper during a breakfast meeting with a customer. And if a trainee came into your office with a problem, you wouldn't half-listen while your eyes stayed focused on your computer screen. Yet, when your husband or children have problems to discuss, do you turn off the television to hear them out? Or do you put them off until the next commercial, and then converse only until regular programming resumes? It's no wonder a recent survey revealed the main complaint children have about their parents is: "They don't listen to me."

THE POWER OF PRAISE

Mary Kay Cosmetics is known for "praising people to success." We think this is so important, we base our entire marketing plan on it.

Unfortunately, the last time many women received applause was at their graduation from high school or college. Women need praise. It's been my experience that a woman will often work for recognition when she won't work for money!

From the moment a new recruit becomes a beauty consultant, we teach her to praise her customers. She learns that a woman who looks prettier on the outside becomes prettier on the inside, too. Not only does the consultant learn to praise people, but after she conducts her first skin care class, her director always looks for aspects of her class to praise. She may ask, "Tell me what I did wrong," but the director replies,

"Let's talk about what you did right." Only after the director highlights her strong points will the new consultant be told where she can improve. Criticism is always sandwiched between two thick, heavy layers of praise.

Our company is also known for awarding pink Cadillacs to top performers. This highly visible, tangible award recognizes achievements in unit sales. The media have described our Seminars held at the Dallas Convention Center each summer as the "ultimate" form of praise, and they're right, because that's exactly our purpose in holding them. Applause is a powerful form of praise. When our top beauty consultants and directors are recognized for their accomplishments in front of an appreciative audience of their peers, the applause ranks among the most meaningful praise anyone can receive.

The pink Cadillacs and glamorous Seminars attract the most attention to our company, but we praise our sales force every day of the year. Recognition given in our monthly magazine, *Applause,* is supplemented by award ribbons, diamond pins, and other tokens of esteem. Our company's employees are recognized for everything from being "employee of the week" to having the best safety record.

Actually, everyone responds favorably to praise. In all likelihood you are either the recipient or the giver of praise (or both) during your working hours. But are you liberal enough with praise for your loved ones?

In many families, only the youngest child receives a steady flow of praise. When a baby first stands on wobbly legs and takes a tiny step only to fall down, we rush to cuddle, and with enough fussing and coaxing, hugging and kissing, the next step is taken. This process continues until a child actually learns to walk. Without this praise, I wonder if we would ever learn. The same praising process occurs when a baby utters the first babbling sounds that, in time, become recognizable words. "Dada" is understood as *Daddy,* and "Mmm" means *Mommy.* Receiving much praise and attention, the baby becomes eager to talk.

As children grow up, parents may cut down on their praising or even stop altogether. Yet the truth is we never outgrow our need for praise. From cradle to grave, we crave it.

Don't let the praise end when your child begins to walk and talk. If you look, there's always something worthy of praise. And no matter how macho you think your husband is, he'll react to praise, too—just as if he were a small child learning to walk!

Every new Mary Kay consultant receives continual praise from her director, who tells her, "You can do it!" These supportive words let her know somebody believes in her—even when she might not believe in herself. With enough repetition of these words and positive reinforcement of her efforts, she develops self-confidence. Children should receive the same encouragement. When they know their mothers believe in them, they develop self-confidence. On the other hand, if a parent repeatedly tells a child that he's shy, he's stupid, he's mean, or he's going to grow up to be a bank robber, he'll probably develop that quality or bring that vision to pass.

When Mattie Dozier debuted as a national sales director in front of a packed audience at the Dallas Convention Center, her husband and family joined her on stage. There were several young children and, as you would expect, some were a bit hard to manage. But for nearly an hour, Mattie's seven-year-old grandson stood quietly, well-mannered and solemn. He was so cute, and I was so impressed by the way he stood there like a little soldier, that eventually I couldn't stand it any longer, and I put the microphone in front of his serious face and said, "OK, young man, is there something you would like to say?"

"Yes," he said. "I'm going to be the first African-American President of the United States."

Knowing Mattie as I do, I wasn't surprised at his confidence and optimism. With all the praise he's given, I am sure that he will accomplish great things in his life.

MANAGING YOUR TIME

In business, we're taught that time is money. But when it comes to being with our families, we can't place a dollar value on an hour. Suffice it to say that our time with them is precious.

If there's one common denominator all working mothers share, it's a lack of time. Again and again, I hear them say, "There's *never* enough time in the day to get everything done."

Just as you make a daily list of your work priorities, make another list of the most important things you want to do with your family. Include things you want to do during the time you spend with your family each night and each weekend.

Again, it's a matter of taking home the discipline you apply to your job. Admittedly, scheduling your activities is easier to do in a work environment than it is at home. In the office, since everyone has appointments to keep and assignments to do, the atmosphere is more conducive to getting organized. A business setting has constancy to purpose as well as fewer distractions.

But the degree of confusion in the home means it's probably even more important to be a good time manager there. Perhaps the main reason we don't organize our off-the-job time better is because we don't have to. At work, our careers are on the line. But at home, nobody supervises us or measures our performance, so we don't feel compelled to use our time effectively. It must be a matter of personal discipline.

Once again, remember Parkinson's Law: "Work expands so as to fill the time available for its completion." Amazingly, if you give yourself a time limit for doing something, you can almost always get it done in that time frame. For example, before there were no-iron shirts, I used to allot myself three minutes to iron a shirt. If I had five shirts to iron, I had fifteen minutes to do the job—period. I timed myself, and I was always able to finish my ironing within my time limit.

I used to allow myself until half past eight each morning to do all my housework before I'd leave for my office. And you know what? I always had everything done by that time. Had I allowed myself until nine o'clock, I am sure I would have spent an extra thirty minutes every morning doing the same amount of work.

We're all capable of doing more when we keep Parkinson's Law in mind. You know what it's like to receive a call from an out-of-town friend who has just arrived on the outskirts of the city and will be at your house in thirty minutes. What do you do? You get your entire house in order in only thirty minutes. Had there been no call, the same job might have taken all day.

A long time ago, one of our directors said something that has become legend throughout our company. She said: "I've been scrubbing my kitchen floor all my life, and it's still dirty!"

PERSEVERANCE

I was listening as a group of directors compared notes about their children. One of them told the following story:

125

It had snowed all day, and Cleveland was blanketed with a fourteen-inch snowfall. The traffic was horrendous and I was running about an hour late when I pulled into our driveway at seven o'clock. I noticed it had been cleared earlier in the day but had since accumulated an inch or two of fresh snow. I rushed into the kitchen to fix dinner for my hungry family. Our nine-year-old, Matthew, the youngest of our three children, was not present. "Where's Matt?" I asked.

My twelve-year-old daughter said, "He came home after school and shoveled our driveway. Then he said he was going out to make some money by shoveling other people's driveways."

"It's been dark for two hours," I said with concern. Turning to my husband, who had already slipped into his bathrobe and slippers, I said, "Honey, I still have my coat on, so would you mind taking over the kitchen while I go out to find Matt?"

I jumped into my car and drove up and down a few streets, looking on both sides for a little boy with a big shovel. I finally spotted him. Matt was just removing the last patch of snow on a long driveway. I sat patiently in the car until he finished, and watched him walk to the door to collect his money. As he headed down the driveway toward my car, I honked and he got in.

"I was worried about you, Matt," I said. "Do you know what time it is?"

"About six or so?" he said sheepishly.

"It's almost seven-thirty, honey."

"No wonder I'm so hungry."

"I bet you made a lot of money today. Debbie said you've been shoveling snow since three-thirty. How many driveways did you do?"

"Just this one and ours," he said.

"In four hours? That's it? What did you do the rest of the time?" I asked.

"I went down both sides of our street and stopped at each house asking everybody if I could do their driveway," he explained. "Finally, I got a customer. I did good jobs on ours and the Wilsons' driveway, right, Mom?"

"You did a wonderful job, honey, and I'm very proud of you," I said, giving his hand a gentle squeeze. "What I'm most proud of, Matt, is that you didn't quit after all those people turned you down. If you never give up when things aren't going your way, you'll turn out to be a great man someday."

"You taught me never to give up, Mom."

"I did?"

"Yeah. I see you go out on cold nights like this, and I've seen you come home when a skin care class wasn't good, but you don't give up, and I shouldn't either."

I looked at the other women to see if their eyes were full of tears like mine, and they were. What a wonderful lesson about life for children to learn from their mothers!

Some say the number one reason salespeople fail is because they can't take rejection. After a few bad days of sales calls, they begin to expect customers to say no. Yet every successful salesperson has had his or her share of rejection. Believe me, I've had plenty of people say no to me through the years. Many times I've said to a group of women, "If we ever decide to compare knees, you will find mine are the bloodiest." In the world of business, and especially in selling, rejection comes with the territory. Nobody likes rejection. But some of us have learned to deal with it.

In all endeavors, there are obstacles to confront. One of the secrets of success is to refuse to allow temporary setbacks to defeat us. In business, we learn this lesson on a daily basis—a lesson that also applies in our personal lives.

A great accomplishment takes a lot of perseverance. If you study achievers throughout history, you'll learn that their successes did not come easily. For example, the world's greatest inventor, Thomas Edison, recorded twenty-five thousand failures in his attempt to invent a storage battery. An interviewer once asked, "Mr. Edison, how does it feel to fail twenty-five thousand times?" He replied, "Young man, those were not failures. I discovered 24,999 ways that the storage battery doesn't work."

In the arts, critics can be brutal. Look at these negative comments about some of the world's most creative people:

"This book is for the season only."
—*New York Herald Tribune*'s review
of *The Great Gatsby* by F. Scott Fitzgerald

"Shakespeare's name, you may depend on it, stands absurdly too high and will go down."
—Lord Byron, 1814

"I'm sorry, Mr. Kipling, but you just don't know how to use the English language."
—1889 rejection letter from the
San Francisco Examiner to Rudyard Kipling

"Strauss can be characterized in four words: little talent, much impudence."
—Cesar Cui, December 5, 1904

"Brahms evidently lacks the breadth and power of invention eminently necessary for the production of truly great symphonic work."
—*Musical Courier,* New York, 1887

"Sure-fire rubbish."
—*New York Herald Tribune*'s 1935 review of
George Gershwin's *Porgy and Bess*

"The Beatles? They are on the wane."
—The Duke of Edinburgh, 1965

The following is a good history lesson on perseverance:

Failed in business	1831
Defeated for legislature	1832
Again failed in business	1833
Sweetheart died	1835

Suffered nervous breakdown	1836
Defeated for speaker	1838
Defeated for elector	1840
Defeated for Congress	1843
Defeated for Congress	1848
Defeated for Senate	1855
Defeated for Vice President	1856
Defeated for Senate	1858

Elected President of the United States. . . . 1860
This is the career of Abraham Lincoln.

TEACHING VALUES BY EXAMPLE

Xerox CEO Paul Allaire tells a good story about learning from a role model. Allaire's father operated a vegetable farm in Massachusetts. "Before the days when refrigerated California vegetables were shipped to the East Coast," Allaire says, "we'd sell our freshly grown goods from a roadside stand. Some farmers put their best-looking vegetables on the top of the basket to hide the small or overripe ones on the bottom, but my father insisted on putting only the finest quality in the basket.

"Later, when Dad operated a sand and gravel business, he would always throw an extra bucket or two on every loaded truck. It really didn't cost a lot, and he wanted every customer to be satisfied and keep coming back. Seeing my father conduct his business this way had a tremendous influence on me. It's a lesson on business relations I've applied throughout my career."

No matter how you go about teaching your children, the values taught by example will leave the most lasting impression. Children pick up so many bad messages outside the family—including from your TV set—that it's up to you as a parent to model correct values for them. As a responsible parent, you

129

owe this to your children; never assume that these values will be taught to them somewhere else.

Again, the do-as-I-say-not-as-I-do message doesn't work. As my uncle used to say, "Little pitchers have big ears." When a young person hears parents talk at the dinner table about cheating on their income tax or padding an expense account, he or she learns a bad lesson. An observant boy absorbs his mother's disregard for the law when he sees her drive over the speed limit. Some families cope with a problem—or, for that matter, celebrate a happy occasion—by drinking. Is it any wonder that the use of drugs has become an extension of the nation's love affair with alcohol? You must set good examples for your children about dozens of issues, and each principle must be demonstrated by your acts, not your words. Children tend to handle life in the way they learned by watching their parents.

Every parent is responsible for setting high standards of integrity for his or her child. In his bestseller *All I Really Need to Know I Learned in Kindergarten,* the Reverend Robert Fulghum states basic values in a language anyone can understand:

> Share everything.
> Play fair.
> Don't hit people.
> Clean up your own mess.
> Say you're sorry when you hurt somebody.
> When you go out into the world, watch out for traffic, hold hands, and stick together.

A WORKING MOTHER'S LEGACY

When you make God and family your priorities, ahead of your career, you will be a positive role model for your children. As every parent knows, children of all sizes scrutinize their mothers carefully; they pick up on *everything*. Your conduct has a tremendous impact on their lives and extends far beyond the home. It carries into the classroom, the playground, and their future lives.

In our organization of more than 375,000 women, millions of youngsters have grown up as "Mary Kay kids" over the past thirty-two years. I would like to share a few stories with you that demonstrate how working mothers with Mary Kay are shaping the lives of their children. Of course, our company doesn't have a patent on this process, but I am most familiar with "our" children's stories.

Julie Rasmussen is president of Mary Kay Cosmetics in Russia. Just thirty years old, this remarkable young woman is the daughter of Kathy Rasmussen, a national sales director in McLean, Virginia. Julie earned a bachelor's degree in Russian studies from the University of Virginia and a master's degree in international affairs from Columbia University.

After just over one year of Julie's leadership, more than five thousand Russian women are selling our products, generating estimated retail sales in excess of ten million dollars. Mary Kay Cosmetics is one of the few free enterprise success stories in Russia since the Iron Curtain was lifted.

In a country riddled with bureaucracy after seventy years of communism, and where the average working woman earns less than one hundred dollars a month, our beauty consultants face enormous obstacles on a daily basis. Julie tells her women: "You don't have a car? You say you have to ride the Moscow metro to make your appointments? You have to carry those heavy bags and boxes? So what? You can do it! I know you can do it! If you think it can't be done, I will show you. Just watch me do it."

When asked where she got her positive attitude, Julie confides, "I developed this thinking growing up watching my mother. She began as a Mary Kay consultant and worked her way to the top. My mother always stressed the power of positive thinking. It became so ingrained in me, as a little girl I remember saying to my friend, 'In our house, you can get in trouble for being in a bad mood.' "

Julie's mother, Kathy Rasmussen, was a schoolteacher before joining the company in 1970; two years later, she became a director. Carefully balancing her family and career over the next twenty years, Kathy became a national sales director in 1992. As a little girl, Julie saw her mother as a shining example of how much a woman can accomplish when she believes in herself.

When Kathy is asked where her daughter got her drive, she says, "I taught Julie and her brother, Eric, to work at something challenging that they enjoy. I showed them that when you work, you get rewarded. If you don't work, you don't get rewarded."

Scores of mother-daughter teams have Mary Kay careers. One team that made company history at our 1994 Seminar is Shirley Hutton and her daughter, Elizabeth Fitzpatrick. Elizabeth had just become a national sales director (NSD), so she and Shirley were the first mother-daughter team to enter the NSD ranks.

Elizabeth is quick to point out that NSD genes are not inherited. What did she learn growing up as Shirley Hutton's daughter? "It's the philosophy that a woman should never compromise or settle for less than she deserves," Elizabeth says. "It was my mother who taught me to think big by her example."

"I was able to open the door for Elizabeth," Shirley is fond of saying, "but like everyone else in this company, she had to do it on her own."

National Sales Director Jan Harris glows when she tells about the time her family moved from Sioux City to Omaha.

132

"We arrived on a Friday," Jan explains, "and my daughter, Josie, was put into a second-grade class that Monday in the middle of the school term. Three days later, I was asked to have a conference with her teacher. I wondered what could be wrong after only three days.

" 'I've taught for eighteen years,' the teacher said, 'and I've never seen anything like Josie in my entire career.'

" 'What do you mean?' I asked.

" 'Well, your daughter just walked into the classroom on Monday morning and went around the room shaking hands with everyone, saying, "Hello, I'm Josie Harris. I'm pleased to meet you." I was so impressed with her, I just had to meet her parents.' "

Jan also tells a wonderful story about her son, Jake. "During his sophomore year in high school, Jake was a standout linebacker on his football team," Jan says. "His coach was so impressed with him that he announced the athletic department was going to make a video of Jake and invite some college scouts in to watch him. But that summer, only three days before a football game, Jake began to have pain in his lower back. The pain was so excruciating, the doctor ran a CAT scan on him. We learned our son had a back disease that could be debilitating if he continued playing sports. Needless to say, that was the end of his football career.

"Jake continued to attend every practice, and he coached the boy who replaced him on the team. At the first game of the season, the team dedicated the game to Jake, and when they won, they carried him off the field. For the entire season, wearing his football jersey and jeans, Jake sat on the bench. In between plays, he held his replacement's hand and continued to coach him.

"After one game, I said to Jake, 'What do you think about him?'—referring to the other boy.

" 'You know, Mom, he's an awesome football player. I'm so proud of him. Isn't it great that he had this opportunity?'

"Jake sees us practice the Golden Rule in Mary Kay," Jan concludes, "and now we're seeing him do the same thing."

National Sales Director Rena Tarbet tells a story about her son, Brian, who worked on a cleanup crew that pulled weeds along the roads to the Dallas–Fort Worth International Airport. "The first day on the job," Rena says, "Brian's boss told him, 'I don't care how many weeds you pull. You just be sure you're pulling one when the big boss comes by.'

"When my son came home from work, he told me what had been said to him. 'I can't believe he told me that, Mom. It made me feel sick to my stomach.'

"My children have seen my work ethic," Rena continues, shaking her head, "and they know to give a fair day's work for a fair day's pay."

Some of the most flattering remarks Mary Kay mothers hear come from an unexpected source: their daughters-in-law. Evidently, our consultants' sons make excellent candidates for matrimony. "I've got the most wonderful husband in the world,"one newlywed recently told her mother-in-law. "Thank you, Mom, for the way you raised him." Of course, it doesn't surprise me that these sons grow up to be fine men who respect women—I know who their mothers are!

When I hear story after story of our wonderful Mary Kay kids, I just beam. So many of them turn into great achievers. Every day, I hear about one who enrolled at Harvard, another who recently graduated from medical school, and so on. Their stories could fill a book. Someone once said to me, "These young people are the real legacy of Mary Kay Cosmetics." I agree!

chapter 10

DEALING WITH
A CAREER CRASH

$\mathcal{M}$ARY KAY Cosmetics was born as a result of a career crash. Mine!

Prior to starting Mary Kay Cosmetics, I had worked my way up, over a period of eleven years, to the position of national training director in a direct sales company. And while I never actually received the title, according to my job description, I was performing all the duties of a national *sales manager.*

Approximately 1,500 women represented the company as salespeople, but I was the only full-time person traveling around the country to open new territories. I spent a week in each city. After I had gone city to city across the United States, we were doing business in forty-three states. Simple arithmetic made it clear that I could get back to each territory only once a year. In spite of my requests, the company refused to give me an assistant. Consequently, without follow-up and management, there was high turnover among the people I had recruited and trained. No wonder the business never seemed to grow.

In near desperation, the company's owner asked, "What do you suggest, Mary Kay?"

"We need an audiovisual program," I said. "It would be used to reinforce what I teach during my annual visit to each territory."

"We can't afford it," he objected.

"We're doing four million dollars in annual sales," I insisted, "and the program would cost thirty-five thousand dollars. I don't think we can afford *not* to have it. Please consider our high turnover before you veto it."

He still refused to put up the money. Then the company president did something that I thought he should have done a long time ago. He hired me an assistant. I was delighted. I'd train this man and ultimately be able to cut down on my constant traveling, which after eleven years had started to get to me.

Less than a year later, after I had finished training my assistant, the company owner promoted him to the national sales manager position—at twice my salary! I was devastated.

That night, I went home and cried my heart out. I wrote my resignation and turned it in the following morning. My boss didn't say a word to me. I cleaned out my office and went home. Had he called me the next day to ask me back, I probably would have stayed with the company. But he didn't.

That's how I retired after twenty-five years in direct sales. I was planning to write a book about the problems I had encountered as a woman in the business world. But after making a long list of the qualities of the dream company I would have wanted to work for, I thought, "Instead of writing a book about how a good company should run, wouldn't it be great if somebody ran one?" And so the idea of Mary Kay Cosmetics was born.

CORPORATE AMERICA DOWNSIZES

In today's changing workplace, a career crash is a common crisis. Crashes have occurred throughout U.S. industry as corporations downsize. With high technology and foreign labor replacing both management and hourly employees, more American men and women find themselves seeking new careers.

Giant U.S. corporations have laid off hundreds of thousands of employees, from the assembly line to the executive suite. For instance, IBM, formerly known as the bluest of the blue chips, has abandoned its full-employment tradition. At its peak in the late 1980s, IBM had nearly 400,000 employees; today, that number has been cut nearly in half. Ironically, the gigantic computer company once boasted that no full-time employee had lost an hour of working time due to a layoff since the Great Depression. IBM can no longer guarantee this job security to its employees. General Motors is another example. In the 1970s, it had 850,000 employees; in 1986, it reduced the number to 407,000, and now its work force is under 250,000.

Companies are sending a new message to the American work force: "We can no longer continue to do business as we did in the past. If we do, our company will not survive. We must find new ways to be more productive with fewer people. If you do not carry your own weight, you are expendable."

These same companies are also telling employees that they must continue to work hard and with devotion to customers. Everyone must remain committed to the company's goals.

In the future, employees will have little or no job security. Only those who add value to a corporation will keep their jobs. Gone are the parent-child relationships that corporate America fostered for generations.

The new arrangement sounds harsh and indifferent to the needs of individuals. Millions of Americans are being squeezed out of positions they thought were theirs to keep until retirement. Those hardest hit are middle-aged and older employees, who, because they are the most expensive to carry on the payroll, are most likely to be let go. Health insurance costs more for older workers, and companies can replace them with younger men and women willing to start at lower wages. Furthermore, companies view younger employees as more adaptable to new technology. Older employees are often considered more difficult to train.

As corporate downsizing proceeds, the "over-the-hill" label is being applied at a much younger age. And employees approaching their peak years, who consider themselves up-and-coming, are seeing their jobs reclassified as unwanted.

So far, downsizing has proved both profitable and productive—at a cost. As you would suspect, employee morale has dropped significantly.

VOLUNTARY CAREER CRASHES

Some people crash their careers on purpose. They reach a point in their lives where they are miserable doing what they do and want a change. Many times they feel that if they don't make a change soon, they could end up spending the next twenty to thirty years at a job they hate.

People who survived the hardships of the Great Depression have emotional scars that remind them to be grateful for the work they have. To them, work is not something to enjoy; you have a job in order to put food on the table and provide a roof over your family's heads. Baby boomers have a different point of view. As they grew up, their parents as well as the media promised them fulfillment in their careers—an ongoing, enriching learning experience.

Throughout our nation's history, each generation of workers has passed along a better way of life to the following generation.

Our grandparents were better off than our great-grandparents and our parents were better off than our grandparents. Eventually, young Americans automatically expected to be more affluent than their parents. Now that may no longer be likely. Many Americans will never be as affluent as their parents, and the affluence of their children is no longer certain to equal theirs. For good reason, people are anxious about long-term financial security for themselves and their loved ones.

In the past, we looked upon job security and guaranteed retirement as entitlements due every American. No longer are they sure things.

The baby boomers are becoming disillusioned. In the real world, work often isn't as fulfilling and rewarding as they were promised. Some find themselves in jobs that don't allow them to use their skills or to do the work they would enjoy. One woman, for example, complained to me, "I'm a people person, but I work at a computer and rarely use my people skills." Another woman said, "I'm creative, but you'd never know it to see me at my job."

Many baby boomers were unprepared to face the drudgery and monotony of their jobs. They did not anticipate the years of noncreative work required to advance to positions in which they could participate in decision-making, so they haven't coped well with the bureaucracy of big business and government.

As they grow older, these people come to understand that they will realize few of their personal ambitions. For the first time in their lives, they see that their chances of sharing in the American Dream are slim. It is a rude awakening.

For an individual with high expectations, a sense of self-worth, and the courage to take charge, the solution is a career change. This kind of person induces his or her own career crash.

STARTING YOUR OWN BUSINESS

The idea of owning a business has long lured people seeking independence. After all, as an autonomous businessperson, you are your own boss: you set your own hours, nobody tells you what to do, and nobody can fire you. These advantages have always attracted entrepreneurs, and with corporate America downsizing, it's no wonder the number of brand-new businesses in the United States today is at an all-time high.

Countless how-to books on starting a business have been written, so there's no need for me to tell you how to open your shop. For those with an entrepreneurial spirit, business ownership may be the best route to go. Of course, you must consider the serious risks. With those risks, however, come rewards—for those who succeed. When I started my own business in 1963 with my entire life savings of five thousand dollars, I had just quit a well-paid job. With everything on the line, if I had failed, I would have had to go back to work for someone else immediately. Mary Kay Cosmetics turned out to surpass my wildest dreams. I never could have predicted that the company would grow to even a fraction of its present size or that it would do a fraction of the good it has done.

If your previous career crashed and you are thinking about starting your own business, I wish you well. But because I don't know you personally, I'm not in a position to say whether it's the right action for you to take. Instead, I'll offer some general advice that may help you make your decision.

First, choose something you will enjoy. This is essential because during the first few years of your venture, you'll be required to put in a great deal of overtime. By the way, if hard work and long hours aren't what you have in mind, don't start your own business. New ventures demand many tedious hours. And though I've often said, "Find something you like to do so much you would do it for free—and somebody will pay you well," you should bear in mind that millions of entrepreneurs don't make any profits their first year in business—and sometimes it takes longer.

Although you should enjoy your work, this alone is not a sufficient basis for starting a new venture. A second reason to go into business is because there is a need for that particular business.

Moreover, you must have some specific knowledge of the type of business you plan to open. I know a well-to-do Dallas woman who wanted to open a restaurant in a resort area. She had no background in the restaurant business; she chose it only because she fancied herself a connoisseur of gourmet food. Hardly what you'd call a strong foundation for a new business, is it? After pouring several hundred thousand dollars of her husband's money into a Continental restaurant in a resort area, she saw its doors close in less than a year. Simply appreciating fine restaurants does not guarantee you can run one. Start with adequate experience. Many things can go wrong when you venture into a field about which you know little or nothing. Rather than learning by trial and error, work for somebody else for a year or more to learn from their successes and failures. Had this restaurateur worked in somebody else's dining establishment for a while, she might have later avoided many mistakes. And she might have discovered, earlier, something else: she didn't even enjoy being in the restaurant business! She learned the hard way that it wasn't as exciting as it appeared on the surface. She had failed to anticipate the long hours the business would require and, after the first month, became bored with being confined from mid-afternoon to one in the morning seven days a week. She also discovered scores of other problems—waitresses who don't show up, customers who fill restaurants with cigarette smoke, zoning laws that interfere with remodeling plans. In short, she learned that the restaurant business was not what she'd hoped it would be.

I've seen many women go into business with too little experience. Like the woman who wanted to own a restaurant because she enjoyed dining out, others open dress shops, jewelry boutiques, antiques shops, and art galleries for similar reasons. One local woman opened an upscale boutique because she wanted to be able to buy her own clothes wholesale. As it turned out, she lost her shirt! She had no idea how much her initial investment in store fixtures and inventory would cost. She found out the hard way. With the money she put into her business, she could have bought the most expensive wardrobe in the entire state of Texas.

Every budding entrepreneur should do his or her share of investigating before jumping in. For instance, when I drive by a certain shopping center in Dallas, every few months I see Grand Opening signs on the same storefronts. Businesses in these spots open and close so regularly, I can't help thinking a person should do some homework ahead of time to find out whether the location or the center has a problem that works against *any* business. My suggestion for any would-be entrepreneur is to talk to former tenants who failed in the same location. Listen to what they have to say before you sign a long-term lease.

The same advice applies to anyone considering a franchise. Investigate each opportunity by visiting existing franchisees, and don't be bashful about asking lots of questions. You may even want to talk to former franchisees who failed, though this may give you the wrong information. Failure may reflect the weaknesses of the individual rather than the business itself.

Buying the right franchise can help you avoid many of the pitfalls of starting your own unique business. A good franchisor provides a proven formula for success, national advertising support, and ample know-how. But not all franchise opportunities are equal. If you choose the wrong one, you could end up working eighty hours a week and making far less than you did at the forty-hour-a-week job you held previously. Remember Sherril Steinman, the woman who became a slave to her own floral shop. Before you invest, investigate.

Some women think the ideal situation is to run a business at home so they can be near their children. A friend of mine, Maggie, opened a desktop publishing business in her home in order to spend time with her young son. After quitting her job and investing thousands in equipment, Maggie found that the deadlines of this business kept her from interacting with her child, almost as if she was still working downtown.

"In the afternoon, he'd come in the door, eager to talk about something that happened at school," she says. "I had to tell him, 'Honey, stand here and talk to me while I keep on typing, because someone is coming to pick this newsletter up at five o'clock.'" Maggie found out the hard way that operating a business in her home did not guarantee quality time with her family.

If you definitely want to fulfill your dream of owning a business, and you have a small nest egg to invest but no real experience, go to work for a period of six months to a year for someone who is already doing what you want to do. Even though you may have to take a reduction in salary from what you currently earn, you'll make it up later with the dollars you'll save by making fewer mistakes on your own. Invest your time to pay the cost of your education.

SECONDHAND CAREER CRASHES

Many years ago, my family moved from Houston to St. Louis when my husband was promoted. Before the transfer, I was making one thousand dollars a month in commissions from a sales unit I had built over seven years. Those commissions ceased when I left Houston, so I virtually had to start all over. As a result of my husband's new job, I experienced a secondhand career crash.

Every day, thousands of men and women across America suffer secondhand career crashes. These occur when a husband and wife both have careers, and one of them is offered a position in another city. When this happens to your husband, the first thing to do is sit down with him and discuss your options. Under such circumstances, assuming you value your marriage, it's imperative that you become actively involved in the decision-making. The two of you may want to consider the following issues:

1. How mobile is your work? Can you transfer your job to another location? Are you easily employable in another area?

2. How much do your earnings contribute to the family's total income? A significant difference between the two incomes may be a major factor. For instance, if you earn much more than your husband and relocation would lower your family's standard of living, the best solution may be for the family to stay put while he finds local employment.

3. What is the long-range potential of his and your careers? For example, your income may increase considerably through future bonuses, advancements, or profit sharing.

4. What are the psychological implications? Money might not be as important a factor as your husband's ego and sense of pride. The same considerations apply to your own emotional needs.

5. How will a move affect other circumstances of your current life? You'll find many factors to consider,

ranging from the presence of school-age children to the need to care for elderly parents.

THERE'S NO SUCH THING
AS SUPERWOMAN

Although many women try, few reach the status of Super-woman. The working mother who thinks she must excel in every facet of her life is attempting to be Superwoman. She toils to reach the top of the corporate ladder, to be named Wife of the Year, to be loved as the world's greatest mom, and to be respected as a dynamic community leader. In other words, she wants it all.

The problem is she has only twenty-four hours a day to accomplish all those things. After meeting the challenges of her job, which may require putting in sixty- to seventy-hour weeks, she simply doesn't have enough time left to do everything else. Something has to give.

Large numbers of women join Mary Kay Cosmetics because it offers a flexible career. Our company was designed to encourage women to work their careers around their families, and our philosophies stand in stark contrast to companies who warn their people that too much concern about their families during office hours will compromise productivity.

In our worldwide organization, we truly have a cross section of women from every field. Although each has an interesting story to tell, I'll focus on just one of them, Dianne Swanson, who previously was an internist. Dianne's story holds particular fascination because doctors are understandably reluctant to change occupations. After the education and training that goes into becoming a physician, medicine is usually a lifelong commitment. Therefore, our ranks include only a handful of doctors.

A few years ago, Dianne took a six-month maternity leave from Mt. Sinai Hospital in Detroit to have her second child. As the wife of a successful businessman, she was able to afford the long absence without pay. "People thought I was crazy for leaving the medical profession," Dianne explains. "'How could you go to school for so long and then just stop?' they'd ask."

But Dianne had recognized her professional dissatisfaction before she even began her leave. "One particular day when I was overloaded with work," she says, "something happened to me. My small daughter was sick with pneumonia, and I wasn't able to be there to care for her. I had to depend on my parents. That's when I realized that I had constantly put off my needs, my family's needs, and the things I needed to do as a mother and wife—all for my profession. It was an everyday occurrence, and just thinking about it frustrated me.

"The more I thought about it, the more I understood I wasn't alone in my frustration. I had observed other female physicians who, after being in the profession for a while, became quite miserable by their mid-thirties. The stress had driven many of my colleagues to divorce. With a job that requires sixty to seventy hours a week, stress accumulates over the years. These women were missing out on so much in life, and I could see I was turning into one of them. The sad part is, nobody cares! Sure, patients say, 'You're such a great doctor!' but that's not enough. It's one thing to be good at your job, but no matter how much you excel, it's not worth sacrificing your family."

On that day when her daughter was sick, Dianne suddenly became aware of the life she was living: "I started to think, 'What's happened to me? I often have to sleep at this hospital. I wake up and I see this hospital. I live at this hospital! I don't remember home!'"

Dianne tells how the practice of medicine has drastically changed over the years. "It's not the dream I thought it was," she says. "Today's rules were never explained to me in medical school. Regulations about what you can and can't do for your patients today sometimes prohibit a doctor from doing what she thinks is best for the patient. Time-consuming paperwork can be overwhelming. Then there's the high cost of malpractice insurance."

Her maternity leave continued past the scheduled six months. Dianne decided to stay home with her children, so she could enjoy them while they were young. Now she and her husband have five children, ranging in age from two to seven.

After three and a half years of staying home to care for her family, Dianne was not bored, but challenge was missing from her life. Then her close friend, Crisette Ellis, a Mary Kay director, told her about the company's marketing plan. "I didn't really understand Crisette's explanation," Dianne says. "But I was her best friend, so I consented when she said, 'Promise me you'll give this two months of your life, and after that, if you're not committed to this business, I'll never mention Mary Kay to you again.'

"When I came home after my first skin care class, my husband greeted me at the door. I put money in his hand and said, 'Look at this!' He was shocked. I had made three hundred dollars, a nice profit for two hours of work. After that first class, I was off and running. Nine months later, I earned the use of a red Grand Am, and two months after that, I became a director. I want to be a national sales director someday, and I am absolutely positive I will reach this goal."

When asked what most attracted her to Mary Kay Cosmetics, the former physician says: "I loved the idea that I could make my own hours around my children's schedule. I'm a very good mother, and my biggest concern as a doctor was that I couldn't be a good mother. Still, I was looking for something to replace my practice, because I did want a career. I prayed to God for some very specific things, and I had six criteria. One: Whatever I was going to do, I had to love it. Two: I wanted to be my own boss.

Three: I wanted an opportunity to earn unlimited income. Four: I didn't want any stress, except for the stress I put on myself. Five: I wanted a challenge—an exciting career. And Six: I wanted to be able to help other people. I suppose this goes back to the same reason I became a doctor."

Dianne sums up her story this way: "As I look back, I had been programmed all of my life to be this superwoman. I had to be everything to everyone. As a doctor, I earned a high income, but at the same time, I wanted to be this wonderful mother and wife. Well, it wasn't possible as a physician, but now, thanks to Mary Kay, I can do it!"

If you're dealing with a career crash, follow Dianne's example by making a list of the criteria for your ideal job. This will help you point yourself in the right direction. Once you know your criteria, you can begin to evaluate which new career path will best suit your needs. And while I'm sure you realize that some compromise may be in order, don't stop searching too soon. My friend Jean, a single mom with two preschoolers, ended her search when she settled for a restaurant manager job that cramped her family time. She was so busy with caring and providing for her young family that she didn't feel she had time to continue looking. Nearly ten years later, she fell into a position with a catering company that offered flexible hours, making it perfect for her family. Yet Jean's ideal career had existed all along, and she could have started it a decade earlier if she'd just kept looking. So be patient and persistent; new career niches are being created every day. It may take some searching to find the unique position you're after, but the effort is worth it.

chapter 11

ADAPTING TO CHANGE

$\mathcal{T}$HE OTHER day I drove by our soon-to-be new headquarters, which occupies more than a city block. As my car sped by, the building seemed to go on and on endlessly.

Looking at the building brought back memories of when our company's entire inventory fit into a small closet. Today, we have five distribution centers in the United States, in addition to our international headquarters.

I began to think about those early days when the business was just getting off the ground. There were only five of us: my sons Richard and Ben, a secretary, a maid, and me. We did everything that is done today by more than 2,500 company employees. We were located in a five hundred-square-foot storefront in Exchange Park, a large bank and office building complex in Dallas. We opened our doors on Friday, September 13, 1963, exactly one month after my husband passed away. I had invested my life savings in formulations, jars, literature, and used office equipment.

Our first expansion occurred one year later, when we moved to 1220 Majesty Drive. We felt as though we had arrived! Richard, Ben, and I each had an office; across the hall was our training room and warehouse. The entire area was five thousand square feet. We tried to be confident that our business would expand and eventually fit into all that space we had leased. But I kept asking myself, "What if it doesn't?"

That same year, we held our first Seminar. I've already told you about the extravaganzas we put on today. But back then, we couldn't even afford to rent a ballroom in a hotel. So we simply rearranged what was stored in our warehouse and convened right there. We did the best decorating job that crepe paper and balloons allow. For dinner we served chicken, jalapeño dressing, and a Jell-O salad. Ellen Notley, a director from Tyler, Texas, baked a delicious cake with "Happy First Anniversary" iced on it.

My secretary, Erma Thomson, even brought her mother to early Seminars. I asked Erma to invite her because we were afraid there wouldn't be enough people in attendance, and we didn't want the large room to look empty. For entertainment, Richard hired a three-piece band, and, after dinner, I acted as master of ceremonies as we recognized the group of about two hundred women who had assembled for our first annual awards night. Hopes were high; the same enthusiasm exhibited at today's Seminars was present that evening, just on a smaller scale. It was a wonderful time.

NOTHING IS
CONSTANT BUT CHANGE

When you think about all the change at Mary Kay Cosmetics during the past thirty years, you can't help but wonder what's next. Back in 1963, when we were launching our little business, the only computers in existence were owned by the government and a few giant international corporations. A company called Univac made a computer the size of a small house. It cost millions in 1994 dollars, and yet its capacity was less than that of a laptop computer today. Of course, it was understood that only somebody with the IQ of a rocket scientist could operate it. Nowadays, computers are as common as television sets and are operated by children.

I could go on and on about what exists today that was once thought impossible. Today, every small business has a photocopier, previously a rarity. And it's hard to imagine what life would be like without car phones and fax machines. I can remember when robots were something we only read about in comic books. Today robotics has become fairly commonplace. Our Automated Storage and Retrieval System (ASRS) is manned by robots that move huge boxes of merchandise around with ease, facilitating the filling of orders with perfect accuracy.

If the past is any indication of the future, technological changes over the next thirty years are going to boggle our imaginations. Lewis Carroll said it well in *Through the Looking-Glass*. The Red Queen cautions Alice: "Now, *here,* you see, it takes all the running you can do, to keep in the same place. If you want to get somewhere else, you must run at least twice as fast as that." The Red Queen's advice is even more appropriate today than when Carroll wrote it. In today's fast-changing, highly competitive world, standing still is the same as moving backward. If you don't go forward, others will zoom right past you.

There are three types of people in this world: those who make things happen, those who watch things happen, and those who wonder what happened. We all have a choice. You can decide which type of person you want to be. I have always chosen to be in the first group. It is important to remember that although change entails uncertainty, it also brings opportunity.

The graveyard of the business world is filled with companies that failed to adapt to change. Only two years after *In Search of Excellence* was published, fourteen out of the forty-three "best run" companies Tom Peters showcased in the book were experiencing financial troubles. According to a *Business Week* study, the reason was "failure to react and respond to change." The long list of corporations that were once household names but no longer exist includes Packard, Studebaker, American Motors, Eastern Airlines, Braniff, Pan American, Railroad Express, and Gimbels. The great Sears Catalog, once an American institution, recently closed down after nearly a century of operation, because it couldn't keep pace with changing times. Following a period of lean years, International Harvester, which has changed its name to Navistar, no longer makes tractors, even though it was the world's leader in the tractor industry for decades. Dairy Queen stands were spread across the country long before the likes of McDonald's, Burger King, Hardees, and Wendy's appeared on the scene.

These companies were highly successful at one time. Where did they go wrong? Each demise can be traced to management's inability to change with the times.

It follows that individuals must embrace necessary change, or they will endanger their careers. Each of us must engage in a lifelong self-improvement program, continually seeking more knowledge and newer methods. We must be open to new ideas and never satisfied with the status quo.

IF IT AIN'T BROKE, DON'T FIX IT

The adage, "If it ain't broke, don't fix it" has been around for years. It means, clearly enough, that you should leave things alone when they are working properly. Or, to put it another way, don't change just for the sake of change.

Since not all change represents progress, it is prudent to think carefully before making a change. Often, Mary Kay

Cosmetics receives suggestions from people in our sales force—an incredible and continual source of ideas. We listen attentively to every suggestion. Yet we have to reject most of them because we can implement only a relative few. Even though we are constantly seeking ways to improve everything the company does, it's impossible—and undesirable—to accept every overture to change.

For example, a woman outside the company wrote: "Now that you are a mature company, don't you think you should get rid of those frivolous pink Cadillacs?" The pink Cadillac has proven to be one of the greatest public relations/advertising ideas we have ever instituted. Even if someone knows little about the company, when they see a big pink car, they think, "Mary Kay!" So while we pursue change, we execute it with caution.

The ability to discern when something new is an improvement requires wisdom. A new method is not necessarily better than a method that has worked successfully for years. Nobody wants to dump a proven method of doing business and risk replacing it with an inferior method. Such a decision doesn't bring progress; it brings regression.

Colonel Sanders, the founder of Kentucky Fried Chicken, firmly believed in his chicken recipe. In fact, he wouldn't allow his franchisees to alter it. The Colonel was right: consumers across the country still choose KFC for its tasty "Original Recipe" chicken. Other franchised businesses must also adhere to standard operating procedures. National franchises strive for uniformity: when a customer checks into Holiday Inn, dines at McDonald's, or drinks Coca-Cola, there should be no surprises. The fact that every product is identical is an essential ingredient in the success formula. These companies will not institute any change until much research has been done.

Some managers assert, "If it's not broken, fix it before it breaks." This school of thought says you should remedy what may go wrong before it's too late to fix. In a highly competitive world, this is good advice. You can't afford the luxury of being complacent; like Alice, if you don't run very fast, you will stay in the same place.

With such a large sales force, Mary Kay Cosmetics must make needed changes swiftly. This means we continually seek to improve our products, service, and distribution to our consultants. As we continue to grow, sustaining high quality and efficiency becomes increasingly difficult, so it must always be foremost in our thoughts. While our size offers certain economies of scale, it can also work against us if we become complacent.

Over the years, our company has witnessed dramatic changes in everything from products to packaging. Like the fashion industry, cosmetics is a field that has no room for the meek and mild-mannered who shy away from change. Women's fashions and cosmetics cater to a fickle consumer. Notice how cosmetics advertisements describe products as "new," "brand-new," "newly introduced," and "the first ever." Women expect and demand up to date products. It's part of our business to anticipate change. We must continually initiate change to maintain a leadership position in our field.

One of our products, Day Radiance foundation, was in our initial product line, but over the years, various improvements determined by new knowledge about skin care have taken away any resemblance to the original product. In the beginning, our skin care products worked well only on women with dry skin, and since many people have oily skin, we lost numerous potential customers. A few years later, we began to manufacture our own products rather than having them made by other companies, and only then were we able to solve many of our early challenges. We continued to improve our product line and are now known for our skin care products for all skin types.

All aspects of our company have always been subject to change. For example, our first sales manual was five pages long, and the first page said only "Welcome." It had little in common with our current guides, brochures, and literature, which have become quite sophisticated.

Our consultants and customers are our best sources as we look for new and better ways to perform. We are blessed to have so many dedicated, intelligent women in the Mary Kay network who share fresh, creative ideas. In addition, our staff conducts periodic focus groups and consumer panels. Before new products are introduced, we convene a volunteer test panel of our directors in order to get their feedback and root out any problems.

Just as our company has a constant drive to keep evolving, so must you as an individual. You can go either forward or backward—this year, this month, this day—but you can't stand still!

WHY PEOPLE RESIST CHANGE

Even when people understand that change is necessary and inevitable, some of them tend to resist it. They may think the new situation or method might not be as good as the old one. These people have a don't-upset-the-applecart mentality. They don't welcome change because it's easier to stay with the status quo.

How many times have you refused to incorporate a change simply because it was not what you were used to? Have you ever heard yourself say, "But we've always done it this way"? At one time or another, we've all been guilty of this behavior. When they were new inventions, automobiles and airplanes met with public opposition. When television sets came on the market, many people vowed never to own one. "Radio stimulates the imagination," critics said. "You don't have to think when you watch TV." Sales representatives for National Cash Register had a difficult time selling the first cash registers. Prospective customers said, "If I buy that contraption, my employees will think I don't trust them." They stubbornly continued to operate out of a cigar box, drawer, or shoe box. Ten years ago, you would have had a hard time finding a retailer who didn't own a cash register. Yet today they are being replaced by point-of-sale terminals.

Here in Texas, it's hard to believe that people once resisted air-conditioning. "Why should I spend money to keep my house or car cold?" they asked. "I've gotten along without it this far." Later, many of the same people resisted computers. A furniture retailer with a sizable business told me, "I don't trust those things, and besides, they're so darn complicated. Our present system for keeping our inventory is working just fine." Talk to him now and you'll learn he has his entire business on-line and feels he couldn't get along without his computer system.

Products we take for granted today were met with suspicion when they first came out. Included are ballpoint pens, electric shavers, home permanents, frozen food, vitamins, and contact lenses. It wasn't long ago that people said, "You mean the lens actually touches the eyeball? No way!"

Change is constant. Cultural, political, and social changes affect the way we live—in our neighborhoods, schools, and offices. Note, for example, the changes brought upon us by the oil embargoes of the 1970s, the AIDS epidemic of the 1980s, and today's crime rate.

But nowhere is change more evident than in the cosmetics and fashion industries. Women's hairstyles, for instance, come and go. Remember frosted hair, cornrows, pageboys? Are the beehives and bouffants of the 1950s coming back? Men are hardly exempt. Their hairstyles fluctuate from crew cut to shoulder length; facial hair—goatees, beards, mustaches—teeters back and forth in popularity; sideburns go up and down nearly as fast as women's hemlines. Men's ties alternate from wide to narrow; their pants seesaw from pleated to pleatless, cuffed to cuffless.

As fashion swings into the future, it seems like ages ago that a well-dressed woman wore evening gloves—as she did in those days before panty hose replaced stockings and garter belts. Many of us remember when a lady never wore pants in the evening and when a well-dressed man always donned a hat and wouldn't be caught dead wearing an earring.

Around the turn of the century, a woman was scorned for smoking in public. Later, cigarette use became socially acceptable, and for a few decades, smoking even made a social statement. Tobacco companies' advertisements told the American public that smoking was sophisticated, and people bought it hook, line, and sinker. In the early 1950s, cigarettes were even promoted as a healthy way to relieve stress. Ads proclaimed: "More doctors smoke Brand X than any other cigarette." In recent decades, people have learned how smoking will damage their health, and attitudes have changed. But this change took many years to come about, and millions of people are still resisting the fact that cigarette smoking is a leading cause of cancer, lung disease, and heart failure.

NEVER CHANGE YOUR PRINCIPLES

Thomas Jefferson once said, "In matters of principle, stand like a rock; in matters of taste, swim with the current." I agree with this advice. We live in a world where everything is subject to change—everything, that is, except one's principles.

In business, every company must have a sound set of principles and, most importantly, adhere to those principles. Mary Kay Cosmetics was founded on our belief in the Golden Rule. We believe in treating people fairly, as we want to be treated ourselves. We apply this basic belief to every decision we make.

In accordance with the Golden Rule, we strive to provide opportunities for women to achieve their maximum potential. And we tell all our consultants and directors that God and their families come before our company—and that whenever they experience a conflict, the company should be put in third place.

These were our beliefs when our sales could be counted on one hand, and more than three decades later, we adhere to them. We are well aware that the world keeps evolving. This evolution has caused our company to experience some incredible changes over the years, and we expect more of these in the future. Products, buildings, advertising, marketing, people—all of these change. We see it happen on a daily basis. Except for principles, everything is subject to change.

If you are thinking about starting your own business, write down specific principles to which your future company should adhere. Entrepreneurs starting businesses rarely follow this advice, but I feel it's never too early to make a philosophical commitment about the direction of your business.

CHANGING PRIORITIES

Priorities change as we go through the stages of our lives. For instance, a young attorney may choose to put aside her ambition to be made a partner in her law firm and elect to work part-time so she can spend more time with her children. When the period of intense need passes, she may again work longer hours to pursue her professional ambition.

A friend of mine was once a high-ranking executive with a pharmaceutical company and had to travel extensively. When her husband retired at the age of sixty-five, she informed her company that she was no longer willing to take trips that required her to be away overnight. After talking with her company's CEO, she elected to take a lower-paying job so she could be with her husband every evening. Even though the couple's combined income took a nosedive, my friend's first priority was being with her husband. They had reached a stage in their lives where being together meant more to them than additional earnings.

When my children were small, I cut back on the number of sales presentations I made so I could spend more time with them. As they became older and less dependent on me, I gradually increased the hours I could spend at work.

Obviously, in times of war, priorities change. During World War II, for example, millions of men and women abandoned their careers to join the war effort. Personal crises in our lives can also cause us to change our priorities. When a serious accident or illness strikes a loved one, it instantly takes precedence over everything else. A tragedy of this nature makes other concerns seem inconsequential. Unfortunately, it sometimes takes a catastrophe for us to grasp what truly matters in life.

For instance, a woman I know in Dallas placed her social life high on her list of priorities. Her memberships in an exclusive country club and an equally exclusive city club were two of her greatest joys. When her husband suffered some business reversals, however, the couple was no longer able to pay their club dues and still afford college tuition for their son and daughter. Their children's education became a priority, and they dropped out of both clubs.

Individuals with good family values are able to prioritize quickly when calamity occurs. They are the people best equipped to survive hard times. And, unfortunately, life is full of hard times.

chapter 12

MENTORING

*O*UR SALES organization has a wonderful built-in mentoring program. Since the consultant who brings a new person into the company can receive a commission (paid by the company) on the recruit's wholesale purchases, the established consultant is naturally inclined to watch over her recruit. She wants to make sure the new consultant gets off to a good start. In time, a strong bond develops between the two women.

The director of the recruiter's unit also serves as a mentor to the new consultant; and further up, so does the national sales director.

If a new consultant's recruiter or director leaves the company, or if the consultant moves to another area, she'll be "adopted" by someone else. Let's say, for example, the consultant moves from Pittsburgh to Miami. Under our adoptee program, a Miami director "adopts" her, taking her under her wing and treating the new consultant as one of her own. Meanwhile, all eligible commissions continue to go the woman in Pittsburgh who originally recruited her.

Our adoptee program is as old as the company itself, and, to my knowledge, it's one of a kind—although we certainly don't have a patent on it. When it was introduced, the "experts" said it wouldn't work. "Why should anybody work to develop an adoptee without receiving any commission on her?" the critics demanded. "Why would I put my time and effort into *your* person with no compensation?" asked salespeople with other companies.

Our thousands of sales directors—a high percentage of whom have recruited consultants who now live in other states—would attest that everyone benefits from our adoptee system. Remember, it's a two-way street. While a sales director may adopt somebody in her city, it's just as likely that one of her consultants will be adopted somewhere else. Over a period of time, the efforts average out. It's possible for a sales director to have more than a hundred adoptees, which means she must devote much time and energy to them. Yet someone else may be watching over an equal number of her consultants who have moved to other areas. In other words, "I'm helping Betty, who belongs to Connie's unit, but Maria, who belongs to my unit, is being helped by Debbie." This system is probably best implemented when a company begins. Introducing it to a going concern might be difficult.

Outsiders may protest: "If Maria becomes involved in Debbie's unit, Debbie surely won't give this new person the same treatment her 'real' unit people receive. Why should Debbie put herself out when she doesn't receive commission on Maria's production?"

When I hear this, I reply, "If you adopted a child, you would not say to her, 'No, you can't have steak tonight. Only my own children can have steak.'" No decent mother would treat her adopted child like this, and neither would our directors with their adoptees.

When a consultant moves to a new area and is adopted by a local unit, she has two wonderful mentors—her original director and her new adoptive director. She gets the best of two worlds.

FINDING A MENTOR

Our company has a plentiful supply of mentors. But outside Mary Kay Cosmetics, finding somebody to serve as your mentor may not be easy.

When I was starting out as a business owner, I desperately needed a mentor, but it was hard to find an appropriate choice. In the early 1960s, not many women held jobs other than low-paid, entry-level positions. Among those who worked, the majority did so for just a few years before marriage, usually in the service sector as a secretary, clerk, or waitress. In comparison to men, they were paid fifty cents on the dollar; few expected a major promotion.

My only mentor was my mother. As a little girl, I learned my work ethic from her. The restaurant where she worked required her to put in long hours, so I always knew that I was expected to work a full day, too. But most importantly, my mother taught me to respect everyone. She said that in God's eyes, we are all equal, and she told me to treat other people just as I would want them to treat me. I have always remembered the ethics I learned as a child.

Good mothers serve as good mentors for their daughters and, fortunately, mothers are in ample supply. But as this is an obvious source, let's concentrate on finding a woman other than your mom to be your mentor. You need someone with success in both career *and* personal life. A prosperous business executive who has not done well as a wife and mother will not be a good role model. A high-paying job does not necessarily indicate a successful life.

To qualify as your mentor, this woman must already have done what you want to accomplish. It's best if you can find a woman who has succeeded in your field, but this is not imperative. A woman who sells real estate can be a mentor to a stockbroker, for example. And if you're opening a retail gift store, you might seek the advice of a woman who owns a dress shop or an art gallery. Every entrepreneur must learn certain basic lessons, so offering the same product or service isn't essential. A high percentage of the obstacles you'll encounter in a new business are not unique to your particular line of work.

It's always easier to ask someone you already know to be your mentor, but you might be surprised by how receptive a stranger can be. You just need a little humility to ask for help. Most successful people are flattered to be asked by either a friend or a stranger. A successful woman doesn't mind lending a helping hand to a novice and, chances are, you'll remind your prospective mentor of herself when she was starting out.

The secret is to find the right mentor. I stress again, a woman with an unhappy personal life may be able to teach you about business, but you'll benefit far more from someone who has balance in her life. Another criterion is similar backgrounds: find a mentor with whom you identify. For example, if you're starting a business on a shoestring, don't choose a mentor who came from an affluent family; she will paint a different picture from the one you see when she relates the tale of her early struggles. Having a mentor who has been retired from business for several years may not work either. The problems she faced in her career may not be today's problems. Even raising a family was much different just a few years ago.

Once you arrange to work with a good mentor, listen to what she advises you to do. After all, there is no point in meeting with her if you do not heed her counsel. Remember that she's there to help you. Be humble and don't pretend you already know everything.

Finally, make sure you choose a mentor who will be available when you need her. No matter how qualified she is, if she's not readily accessible to guide you, she's not the right mentor.

THREE COURAGEOUS WOMEN

Our company has more than ninety national sales directors and more than 7,500 directors who are wonderful mentors for the beauty consultants in our sales organization. Among these women are three highly courageous individuals: Rena Tarbet, Shirley Oppenheimer, and Sharon Coburn. All are cancer survivors.

I told you earlier about Rena's ten-year bout with breast cancer. It metastasized to bone cancer originating in the sternum and later spread into her skull, left shoulder, and lower back. During that time, Rena was in and out of the hospital, receiving repeated doses of chemotherapy and cobalt while undergoing extensive surgery. Today, Rena is considered a medical miracle; the odds against her surviving were staggering.

Throughout her terrible illness, Rena pursued her Mary Kay career and was able to work her way up to the rank of national sales director. In addition to attaining professional success, she has served as a fabulous inspiration to our entire sales organization. When asked how she coped, Rena answers, "I never gave up hope. I believe without hope there is no life. I never lost sight of the light at the end of the tunnel. That's what kept me going back for those chemo treatments.

"I believed that God wasn't through with me yet," she continues. "I understood that God kept me on the earth because that was where He could use me best. This thought became my prayer, and I said to Him, 'Lord, if you can best use me when I'm sick, that's fine. I'll take chemo the rest of my days, whatever length of time that may be.'

"As the Apostle Paul tells us in the Bible, he had a thorn in the flesh. He prayed many, many times to God to remove the thorn, but for whatever reason, He didn't choose to. But Paul continued to serve the Lord. I visualized my cancer as my thorn in the flesh.

"In time, I began to realize that God was using me to reach other women. They saw how I endured my illness—with courage, grit, and determination. In spite of the chemo, I had a high level of energy. I can't begin to tell you how many women have said to me, 'I was feeling sorry for myself because of my personal troubles, but then I looked at you and realized I had nothing to complain about. If you can do what you've done, I can overcome my problems.'"

Another cancer survivor and one of our leading directors, Shirley Oppenheimer, lives in San Antonio. She has endured twelve operations in the past three years. Incredibly, during this time, Shirley missed only two Monday-night unit meetings. She claims those Mary Kay get-togethers gave her the boost she needed to get through her illness. "I knew that being around women who were setting goals and achieving them would be good for my spirit," Shirley says. "I figured their excitement and enthusiasm would have a positive effect on my attitude."

It's just like Shirley to say how much she received from these meetings. But according to other women who were there, she always gave more than she received. Like Rena, Shirley claims, "God's not through with me yet. I knew I had to go on, because I have a lot more to share with other people."

Shirley tells women at those unit meetings, "We all have problems and challenges in our lives. What if I were to ask each one of you right now, 'What is the biggest challenge you're experiencing?' Whether it's health, the loss of a loved one through death or divorce, or whatever it may be, if everyone here wrote down her own problem and we put them all on this table and I asked you to pick one of them to be your own, do you know what? In all likelihood, each of you would choose your very same problem to take home when you leave here tonight. You see, we all have problems, but what counts is how we work through them. It's a matter of having the right attitude."

Shirley feels that her cancer has made her a stronger person. "After what I've gone through," she explains, "I'm able to look anyone straight in the eye, hear her problem, and say, 'I know you can get through it,' and then add, 'And here's how you do it.' The beauty of it is that these women saw me walk away after my fight with cancer. They sat beside me at the unit meetings. They saw me conduct my business on the phone from my hospital bed. And they saw that I had surgery on May 31 and still attended Seminar in July. They know that if I can do what I did, they're capable of overcoming their own obstacles."

A third survivor of cancer is Sharon Coburn, a senior sales director who lives in Owen Sound, Ontario, a small community north of Toronto. In 1989, at age thirty-five, a large tumor was removed from Sharon's bowel, and the doctor told her she had six months to live. Sharon survived, even though the cancer had spread to her liver, lungs, esophagus, and bladder. In June 1994, after she had undergone surgery for the fourth time in five years, it was determined that her abdominal core was infested with cancer.

"Prior to this last bout," she says, "my oncologist looked at my file and said, 'Sharon, the woman in this file is a person who is dying or is practically dead. But *you*—when I look at you, none of this makes sense. It's as if I have the wrong woman's folder.' Of course, he was referring to my attitude, because, then and now, I refuse to give in to my illness.

"After my last surgery in June, once they saw what was inside me, they closed me up again. I was told the cancer had spread to such an extent there was nothing more that could be done. 'Go home and rest,' they told me, 'and have a good life.'

"They just wrote me off as dead, but I won't allow myself to be defeated. Sure, there are days when I'm so sick I can't work, but there are lots of days when I can. Each morning, I look in the mirror, and just as I have been taught throughout my Mary Kay career, I tell myself, 'You're happy, and you're terrific, Sharon. With God's help, you are going to have a great day!'

"Sometimes, it takes a lot to get going," Sharon admits. "I'm generally nauseated in the mornings and in a lot of pain, so I take my 120 milligrams of morphine, which I do twice a day, and I'm ready to go. My husband, Jim, who's Owen Sound's traffic controller, walks home from his office around noon and has lunch with me. Sometimes, when I'm not feeling strong enough to get dressed, Jim pitches in and makes our lunch. I'm blessed with a wonderful, loving husband, and I consider myself a lucky woman."

Despite her illness, Sharon has been sensational in her Mary Kay career. In 1994, her unit sales were nearly $600,000. It was an incredible feat considering she is able to work only about four hours each day, starting at around one o'clock in the afternoon. "Now and then, when I'm feeling up to it, I'll go out for an evening appointment," Sharon says. "But more recently, I've been inviting women to my home, where I conduct unit meetings as well as skin care classes."

Sharon claims that her illness has forced her to become a stronger woman. It has also compelled her to work more intelligently. "I have 130 women on my team," she notes, "and when they see what I am able to accomplish in three to four hours a day, they realize how much more they can do because they're healthy.

"I used to travel one week out of the month to my team scattered around Canada, but now traveling is very difficult. Instead, I have to conduct that part of my business over the telephone. But my Mary Kay career is working fine, and it's teaching other women to appreciate how much they have. I'm constantly telling them that we must all realize how brief and precious life is."

Sharon also tells the women in her unit that they must not give in when they encounter minor setbacks: "If a skin care class has to be postponed, so what? Or if somebody disappoints you, stop feeling sorry for yourself, and go back to work."

Like Rena and Shirley, Sharon inspires everyone she touches. I have great admiration for these three courageous women. May God continue to bless them.

THE JOY OF MENTORING

Most successful people will tell you: "If it were not for the help of other people, I wouldn't be where I am today."

I believe that everybody who accomplishes something great has had help from someone. Somebody, somewhere, provided a spark of inspiration, offered a challenge, or held out a hand along the way. I know it's not always possible to help these people in return, but you can do for others what was done for you. We owe this to the world. By repaying our debts, we become strong. The wonderful feeling that comes from helping people gives meaning to your accomplishments. If you don't help others, your own success means less; it may even feel hollow.

A successful writer told me that her first novel was rejected by twenty-two publishers. "I didn't think I'd ever find a publisher, Mary Kay," she says.

"One day, I saw an author at a book-signing party and stayed around until everyone else left. After I finally got up the nerve to introduce myself to the author, I told him about my rejection slips. I told him I didn't think anyone was reading my manuscripts. 'You must have a good editor,' I said. 'Perhaps if you gave me the name of your editor, I could send my manuscript to him, so somebody in the publishing industry would read my book.'

"I wasn't prepared for what the author said next: 'It took me ten months to find my publisher, and I went through misery and anguish before I sold my first manuscript. Why should I make it easy for anyone else?'

"I didn't say a word. I just walked away feeling sorry for that author. Later that night, I vowed I would have an entirely different attitude if I ever got my first book published. 'I've gone through so much misery and anguish for so long,' I thought, 'that if I become published, I'll do whatever I can to help others avoid the pain I'm enduring.' Well, Mary Kay, a few weeks later, I received an acceptance letter from a publishing house, and since then I've had nine novels published, some of them bestsellers. I've since helped at least a dozen writers get their first work published, and I can't begin to tell you the joy I receive each time this happens."

If a mentor has helped you achieve your goals, extend a helping hand to someone who approaches you to be her mentor. And if no one approaches you, resolve to seek out someone whom you can assist. Moreover, even if you haven't had the help of a mentor, be a mentor to someone else. And when that relationship has served its purpose, continue to help woman after woman. While it won't—and shouldn't—be your intention, you'll receive much more than you give.

As with every woman who joins our sales organization, each of our more than ninety national sales directors started as a beauty consultant. These women have climbed to the pinnacle of success and know every facet of our business. Each is a highly skilled professional. Each is also a mentor to thousands of women in her own right. Just as I have mentored these women, they now serve as mentors to many others.

And just as I founded this company on a strong belief in the Golden Rule, our national sales directors practice it every day of their lives. I have spent enough time with them to know that they have the same priorities I do. And as I have encouraged each one to strive to achieve her full potential, today I see them encouraging other women to do the same. I have watched our national sales directors grow into wonderful role models. If I were a young woman just starting my career, I would choose these women to mentor me. I am very proud to see them serve as mentors to so many.

Years ago, I worried about what would happen to the company if I were no longer involved. I had a deep concern for all of the people associated with Mary Kay Cosmetics. Knowing the company had helped so many women develop their talents and realize their goals, I wanted to be certain everything would continue to be available to still more women long after I am gone. I no longer worry. When I look at our national sales directors and the outstanding directors who are daily joining their ranks, I know my legacy is assured.

chapter 13

A GOOD SELF-IMAGE

EVERY NOW and then, a brand-new Mary Kay beauty consultant will come into my office with so little confidence she can barely tell me her name. Six months later, after encouragement and praise from her recruiter and director, she'll come back a dynamic person, so confident and polished I have trouble believing she is the same woman.

I heard one of our women say, "When I first began my Mary Kay career, I was terrified to speak in front of even a small group of people. I never thought I'd make it through my first skin care class. I was so shy, I couldn't lead in silent prayer!" A while later, the same woman repeated the same remark—on a stage in front of eight thousand people. This time, she was radiant and bubbled with enthusiasm. She told the audience that anything was possible if they committed themselves to doing it.

What causes such transformation is the loving attention these women receive from their directors, who praise them to success. When a woman with a negative self-image comes to feel good about herself, she changes into a different person.

The women who use our products undergo this same transformation. Again and again, the woman who knows she looks good starts feeling better about herself.

I have often said that we are in the self-image business because we build high self-esteem in both our skin care consultants and our customers. I believe this outlook accounts for a great part of our company's success.

THE MAGIC OF BELIEVING

In his classic book, *Think and Grow Rich,* Napoleon Hill wrote, "Whatever the mind of man can conceive and believe, it can achieve." This famous line on positive thinking applies to everyone. Believing in yourself is the vital ingredient in determining your success. Every achievement, big or small, begins in your mind. It starts as a thought. Your self-image comes into play as you act on that thought. Confidence stimulates your ability to perform.

Every day we see how a positive self-image makes an important difference in a person's performance. I once walked into a car dealer's showroom with the intention of buying a new car. My mind was made up. I knew exactly what I wanted, and the salesman had only to fill out the order.

After we took a brief demonstration ride, the salesman mumbled on and on about the car's high-performance engine and its rating in several automotive magazines. He made no attempt to close the sale. Eventually, I began to have second thoughts, and I left the showroom without making the purchase. The salesman's lack of confidence was contagious: as he hemmed and hawed, I started hemming and hawing, too. Soon, I lacked the resolve to buy the car.

That night I felt frustrated. I wanted to buy a car but couldn't, because the salesman didn't close the sale. I realized the salesman must have had such a poor self-image that he anticipated my decision not to buy; so rather than having to face rejection, he avoided closing the sale altogether. The following day, I went to another dealership where the salesman didn't hesitate to ask for the order. He believed in himself and *knew* I was going to buy. And I did.

Imagine a situation where two women from similar backgrounds apply for the same position. They possess comparable skills. However, one has ample self-confidence while the other is a shrinking violet with so little confidence she has trouble looking another person in the eye. The one who is unsure of herself even has difficulty expressing herself. Is there any question which of the two will be hired?

In another scenario, a prospective business owner applies for a loan at her local bank. Picture a woman who is well dressed, fully prepared, and knows her business backward and forward. Imagine how self-assured she appears to the loan officer. "I've studied your proposal," the banker tells her, "and frankly, I don't know a great deal about the graphic design field. But I have to assume you do. What I do know is people, and I believe in you. I'm going to approve this loan application because I don't invest in businesses, I invest in people." This loan might have been denied had the woman not expressed confidence in herself as a business owner. After all, why should a banker have confidence in a business in which the owner appears to have no confidence?

In selling, there are mornings when everything you do works like a charm. By midmorning, you have made two sales, and you're positive the next prospect is a sure thing. Like clockwork, you make the sale. By early afternoon, your confidence is so high, you can sell to anyone. By the end of the day, you've broken all your past sales records. When you stop to analyze how it happened, you realize that *you made it happen* with your certain belief that it would. Whether you're in sales, sports, business, or law, those good days don't occur by chance. They result from attitude.

Years ago, while I was conducting a training session in Houston, I talked about the importance of having a good self-image. "When you have confidence in yourself, you'll create a positive buying environment," I said. "By having your hair, nails, and makeup done properly, you'll feel good about yourself, and this will come through to your customers. If you don't have a dress that makes you feel like a million dollars, go buy one. If you have just one dress in your closet that makes you feel wonderful—the one you receive compliments on whenever you wear it—wear that dress to every skin care class until you can afford to buy another one."

In the audience was a consultant who had never held a hundred-dollar skin care class. Even though she and her husband were having hard times financially, and she hadn't bought a new dress for three years, she bought one as soon as the session was over. That night she conducted her first hundred-dollar skin care class.

Evidently, she decided that if one new dress was good, two would be better. She purchased another dress before her next skin care class. Again, she held a hundred-dollar class. She bought a third dress and, for the third time in a row, held a hundred-dollar class. Having gone three for three, she was convinced she had found the secret to success. At the meeting on the following Monday, she announced, "Buy a new dress and you're sure to have a hundred-dollar skin care class!"

Obviously, buying a new dress wasn't the reason for her newfound success. Her improved appearance made her feel confident. In turn, she was more enthusiastic and believed she would succeed. I've seen many salespeople who had lucky suits or ties; when they wore these items, they had outstanding days. Of course, the customer doesn't buy because she likes a salesperson's dress or tie. The customer buys because a salesperson with a good self-image *knows* he or she is going to make the sale.

A young girl putting on her first prom dress glows with the certainty that she looks beautiful, and we all have a similar radiance when we know we're looking our best. While clothes may not make the woman, they certainly have a strong effect on her self-confidence—which, I believe, does make the woman.

BREAKING YOUR BELIEF BARRIER

Fifty years ago, it was generally believed that no one would ever run a mile in under four minutes. Some runners came close, but most felt it wasn't physically possible for a human being to run that fast. Then, in 1954, Great Britain's Roger Bannister ran a mile in 3 minutes and 59.4 seconds. Three months later, in Vancouver, in what was billed as the mile race of the century, Roger Bannister ran against John Landy. Bannister clocked in at 3 minutes, 58.8 seconds against Landy's 3 minutes, 59.6 seconds.

Once other runners knew the four-minute barrier for the mile could be broken, they began breaking it rather routinely. Today, the world record for the mile is down to 3 minutes, 46.32 seconds. But until Bannister proved a mile could be run in under four minutes, the present record was considered impossible.

Too often, we limit ourselves by putting up imaginary barriers. Over the years, I have seen women do this more than men. Men typically try to bluff their way through new or difficult situations, even if they actually doubt themselves, while many women openly disbelieve their own God-given abilities.

Some women qualify everything they say with "if I can," "I hope," and "maybe."

To overcome self-doubt, these women have to be continually encouraged. Each Mary Kay beauty consultant hears "You can do it. I know you can!" again and again until she believes in herself. If she doesn't come to believe in herself, she'll never accomplish much, because she'll probably never even take the first step.

This is why we begin simply by praising everything a new consultant does well. For instance, she receives a ribbon after her first hundred-dollar class (which, by today's standards, is a minor achievement). More ribbons are given for classes exceeding two hundred dollars, three hundred dollars, four hundred dollars, and so on. With each ribbon, her self-esteem goes up another notch, and, eventually, she is able to stand up at a unit meeting and talk about her achievement. During a Mary Kay meeting, anyone who feels she has done something exceptional stands up and talks about it. Not only does voicing her success give her confidence, it inspires other women. They think, "If she can do it, I can, too."

When I met Rubye Lee-Mills, she was perhaps the shiest person I had ever seen. She came from Atlanta to Dallas for a week in 1969 as a director in qualification, and whenever I would say, "Good morning," she'd duck her head, too bashful to reply. I remember telling one of our vice presidents, "Rubye's so shy, I don't see how she's ever going to make it."

Years later, Rubye told me in her soft Southern accent how she started her Mary Kay career: "I came into the business because I loved the products. My goal was to teach skin care because I knew it was so good for women's skin. I wanted only to teach, not sell. I was happy as long as I could show the products to just one person. I did it only as a hobby and never intended to make a career out of Mary Kay. It was something I could do at my leisure without being away from my children for very long.

"I was so sold on the product that it was all I talked about. My friends and family were getting bored hearing me talk so much. So I challenged myself to become a director so I could make money to prove to them how good the company is. Once I started to recruit other women, I dedicated myself to helping them succeed. Then something wonderful happened. I became so involved in their goals and aspirations, I forgot about my own fears and inhibitions. As the other women grew, so did my confidence."

Rubye went on to become a national sales director, and today she is a polished public speaker, comfortable in front of large audiences.

LOOKING GOOD AND FEELING GOOD

Sometimes a woman comes reluctantly to a skin care class. From the way her arms are folded and from the expression on her face, the consultant can see that this woman doesn't want to be there. When asked to participate, she says, "I'm too old," or, "I'm too ugly," and "There's nothing you can do about it."

She obviously isn't feeling good about herself! So the consultant tries to persuade her gently. "Your face will feel soft and nice," she coaxes. "Please try. I know you'll enjoy it."

If the consultant exercises tact and finesse, the woman will usually consent to having a facial. Once her skin looks and feels better, she'll agree to putting on makeup. One hour later, you can't pry the mirror from her hands. Why? She looks in the mirror and likes what she sees. She feels pretty, and that makes her feel good about herself. Her self-esteem rises, and when she goes home, she holds her head high and walks with an air of confidence. She looks as though she has just experienced a personal triumph or accomplishment.

While critics argue that a woman's appearance is only superficial, I disagree. When a woman changes from an ugly duckling into a beautiful swan, something inside changes, too. Outer beauty kindles inner beauty.

When a woman has been seriously ill, there's one sure sign that she is on her way to recovery. She'll start fixing her hair and putting on her makeup. When I visited my mother at her nursing home in Houston, I knew she was feeling better when she asked, "Did you bring your beauty case, sweetheart?"

"Yes, Mother."

Her second question was predictable: "Honey, would you please fix my face?"

Years ago, Mary Kay Cosmetics participated in a scientifically controlled study at the Golden Acres Nursing Home in Dallas. My personal physician at that time, Herman Kantor, a member of the nursing home's board, told me that the home wished to conduct an experiment to determine whether a positive change in a woman's mental attitude could result from improving her appearance. "Since Mary Kay consultants conduct skin care classes to improve a woman's self-image," he explained, "we would like your company to participate in our research." Dr. Kantor added that a team of physicians, including a psychiatrist and a psychologist, would evaluate the entire program.

The home had 350 residents, and researchers needed a minimum of sixty volunteers to have an adequate base. In the beginning, few women were willing. "You're twenty years too late," they said. They claimed to have little interest in their appearance; they preferred to watch television all day or even stay in bed. A beautifully equipped recreation room was nearly empty all the time. They lacked enthusiasm, and just thinking of working with them was almost depressing.

We did, however, eventually persuade sixty women to participate. At seven o'clock each morning, our volunteers helped them with their basic skin care and makeup application.

Two months later, I went back to the nursing home to see how the program was progressing. I couldn't believe what I saw! Those formerly listless women were up and about, alert and bright-eyed, and decked out in their finest clothes and jewelry.

The study included only women because no one thought men in their seventies and eighties would be interested in skin care and cosmetics. But when I walked down the halls on that visit, male residents followed me and said, "You're playing favorites. We demand equal rights. We want to be in the program, too."

Six months later, the study was concluded. Researchers had documented a change in nearly every participant. These residents had begun getting up early in the morning. "Where's my Mary Kay volunteer?" was one of the first things on their minds. The recreation center was now full of men and women engaged in all types of activities. In general, they seemed to exhibit a renewed gusto for life.

To express their gratitude, the home's residents gave a luncheon in my honor. Had I not known better as I looked around the room at the men and women in attendance, I would have thought it was a different group of people from those I observed during my first visit.

After lunch, Dr. Kantor's wife took me on a tour of a ward where individuals with serious mental problems lived. Mrs. Kantor wanted me to meet one elderly woman in particular. I remember her well. This tiny, frail woman had lost her ability to reason and was secured in a geriatric high chair much of the day so she could sit upright without falling out. For several years, I was told, she had sat there day after day with her head resting on the tray. During this time, she didn't speak a word or appear to recognize anyone. Just the same, the doctors included her in the experiment. As Mrs. Kantor explained, each morning, a volunteer held this woman's head up and applied her skin care treatments and makeup. During these times, the volunteer spoke soothingly to her, giving her the same tender loving care we give our customers.

"This is Mary Kay," Mrs. Kantor said, as she knelt beside the woman whose head rested on the tray. "Mary Kay is the lady who gave you your cosmetics."

To our astonishment, the woman lifted her head to look at me, and a faint smile flickered over her face. It was the first reaction she had shown in three years! That one gentle smile was all I needed to know that the program was worthwhile.

WHICH CAME FIRST,
THE CHICKEN OR THE EGG?

When you think about it, none of us is much different from that woman who had a successful skin care class after buying a new dress. Both women and men feel better when they are all dressed up and looking their best.

When you feel good because you look good, people respond to you positively. While some contend that you feel good because people treat you well, I believe that feeling good about yourself stimulates a positive reaction toward you. It's the old question: Which came first, the chicken or the egg?

What woman hasn't dashed to the grocery store on a Saturday, wearing jeans, no makeup, and curlers in her hair? Any woman doing this knows she looks terrible and will do everything possible to avoid running into somebody she knows. If she were to go shopping for a dress, she'd probably have a difficult time getting anyone to wait on her. Salesclerks would treat her as if she were invisible.

Had the same woman come to the store neatly put together in a nice outfit, the treatment she would receive from salesclerks would be entirely different. Is it simply the clothes? The makeup? The hair? Or is it her self-assurance and poise that generate the positive response?

A book is often judged by its cover, and people do judge you by your appearance. Whether you're selling a product, applying for a job, vying for a promotion, or running for public office, people evaluate your ability by your appearance. They appraise not only your grooming but the air of confidence you project, which is a reflection of how you feel about yourself.

There is certainly more to a person than appearance. But you still get only one chance to make a good first impression!

ONE STEP AT A TIME

When outside guests and media people attend a Mary Kay Seminar, I frequently hear: "Your people are all such terrific speakers. What kind of public speaking course do you give them?"

"I agree, they are wonderful," I answer, "but we have no public speaking course. They learn by osmosis."

It's been said that death and public speaking are a human being's two worst fears—and not necessarily in that order! Insecure people quake at the thought of addressing an audience. Their fear isn't actually of speaking but of rejection. They tremble to think they might be rejected by a large group of people. The larger the group, the more overwhelming the anticipated rejection.

Rarely can an individual with no prior experience step in front of a full auditorium and deliver a notable speech. Great public speakers generally start by addressing small audiences, and then, over a period of time, they develop enough self-confidence to feel at ease before larger groups. In our case, they learn first to speak in front of three to five people at a skin care class.

National Sales Director Arlene Lernarz never dreamed she would one day speak in front of a packed house at the Dallas Convention Center. "I didn't have the confidence to second a motion at a PTA meeting," Arlene admits, and she jokes, "Dick stopped taking me to the football games because I was so self-conscious; when the team huddled, I thought they were talking about me." But when Arlene first joined Mary Kay, her stage fright was no laughing matter.

"I'd get butterflies in my stomach even when I held a skin care class for only a handful of women," Arlene says. "But with all the praise I received, I began to feel confident. Yes, we do praise each other to success. Everyone is cheered whenever she does something well, no matter how insignificant it may seem. It took me a while to get up the nerve to talk at those first sales meetings, but before too long I was able to lead one. By the time I was asked to speak at Seminar, I had made so many speeches to small- and medium-sized groups of Mary Kay people, I knew I could address *any* audience."

Kathy Helou, another national sales director, used to live in her husband's shadow. "My husband owned a nightclub in Toledo where he was known as 'Mr. Entertainer,' " she says. "When I went to his club to watch him sing, I'd sit in the very last row. I was afraid if I sat up front, I might get introduced to the audience. When I was introduced to anyone, I always identified myself as 'Mrs. Entertainer.' I didn't have enough self-esteem to say, 'I'm Kathy Helou.' But once I began to have small successes as a skin care consultant, my confidence level rose. I started to grow, one success at a time. By the time I was a director, I felt comfortable conducting a unit meeting for a small group of women. Today, I love to speak in front of every audience, large or small, and I tell new consultants, 'I was where you are, and I know how you feel, because I felt the same way.' "

Sweaty palms and running to the bathroom are what National Sales Director Darlene Berggren once associated with public speaking. "The only time I'd addressed an audience before was in college speech class," she says. "My husband belonged to a Toastmasters Club, and for the life of me, I couldn't understand why he or anyone else would enjoy being called on to speak spontaneously. 'How awful,' I'd think. 'What a terrible thing to have to do.'

"But at my Mary Kay meetings, I stood up to tell the other women something good that happened in my week, and a little bit at a time, I got stronger."

Denny, Darlene's husband, has told other husbands at Mary Kay functions: "Forget about the money, the diamonds, and the pink Cadillacs. Sure, all that is wonderful. But if the only thing my wife got from Mary Kay is self-confidence, we're both way ahead."

Being well-prepared is a major contributor to self-confidence. Do your homework before you make a sales call; decide exactly what you want to say before you deliver a speech; develop your professional skills through education, training, and experience. All these actions will increase your level of confidence.

A WOMAN'S SELF-IMAGE
AND HER FAMILY

The wife and mother sets the mood for her family in the morning. If she gets up feeling grumpy, her husband and children may leave the house with a negative attitude. Imagine a family starting their day with a woman who comes to the breakfast table in a bathrobe, hair in curlers, and face undone, mad at the world because she had to get out of bed.

Now picture this same exhausted woman at day's end, coming home from a job she can't stand, after being told off by an irate customer and having an argument with her supervisor. At the very least, her battered self-esteem will put a damper on her whole family's dinner experience.

Wouldn't you prefer your children to see a mother who gets up feeling glad and perky? This cheerful woman hums a tune while she fixes breakfast for her family and gives them hugs and kisses as they leave the house. Whether she realizes it or not, she has just set the tone for her husband's day at the office and her children's day at school.

Since a woman's husband and children are the most important people in the world to her, shouldn't she want to look her best for them as well as for herself? And shouldn't she want to radiate self-esteem when she's with them?

To illustrate the importance of a woman looking her best for her family, let me tell you about a man who called me at my office. As soon as I picked up the receiver and before I could say a word, he declared, "Mary Kay, I called to thank you for saving my marriage."

He was a stranger to me, and I had no idea what he meant. "My wife and I have been married for eight years," he continued, "and when we first met, she looked like she was right out of the pages of *Vogue*—every hair in place, stylish clothes, a beautiful face, and a nice figure. But when she became pregnant with our first child, she was sick almost the entire nine months. She seemed to lose interest in her appearance. Then our second child came along, and the cycle repeated. She rarely fixed her hair or made up her face. It got to the point, Mary Kay, that when I came home at night, she would be standing in the kitchen with one child hanging onto that tiresome housecoat and another screaming in her arms.

"About two months ago, she was invited to a Mary Kay skin care class and bought twenty-eight dollars worth of products." (I could tell that this amount sounded like the national debt to him.)

"But," he said, "the woman who sold it to her really did a good job. My wife probably thought I'd be upset if she spent twenty-eight dollars on cosmetics and didn't use them, so when she got home, she put them on her face. As soon as she saw the improvement, she had to do her hair and get dressed. When I got home that night, she looked terrific! It had been so long since I'd seen her looking that way, I'd forgotten how beautiful she really is. And the best part is that she now fixes her face and hair and gets dressed *every* morning. Besides that, she's lost twelve pounds. I've got my old girl back. We're falling in love all over again, and it's all because of you."

Another man's wife reentered the job market after a fourteen-year absence. "When our youngest daughter went off to college," he tells the story, "Linda needed something to fill the void in her life. She was in a rut and was convinced nobody would hire an 'over-the-hill,' forty-six-year-old woman. Of course, I knew this wasn't true. Not only was Linda a terrific mother and homemaker, she had taught herself to use a computer to help the kids with their schoolwork, and she was active in community activities that required good people skills. I kept telling her, 'You have a lot to offer.' But when she looked in the mirror, she saw a has-been.

"I convinced her to set up an appointment with an employment agency," the husband continues. "The woman who was her counselor suggested Linda would have a better chance if she would buy herself a smart business suit for interviewing. 'And while you're at it,' the woman said, 'why not do something different with your hair?' I have to admit Linda had not changed her hairstyle for a long time. Linda followed the advice, and it was just what she needed to have the confidence to make it through the interviews. When she looked in the mirror and saw herself in her new suit and haircut, she no longer saw someone who was 'over-the-hill.' After a few interviews, Linda landed a job as an office manager at a law firm, and in the following days, her self-esteem skyrocketed. Within months, she was literally transformed into a new woman. She believes in herself now, and her new self-confidence is contagious. She even sings around the house. I don't know how to explain her transformation, but it makes me feel better about myself, too."

Many times when you give your self-esteem a boost, you do the same for your family's morale. One friend of mine went back to school for her master's degree after her children left the nest. Her beaming husband had the video camera rolling as she walked down the aisle to pick up her diploma. Her achievement is now a source of lively conversation at family get-togethers.

Another mother with three grown sons began taking art classes after work. "I've always had a secret desire to sculpt," she explains. "I felt I might have some innate talent, but there was never time to pursue it. Now, after four years of study, I'm having my first exhibit. Bruce has invited all his coworkers to the opening, and the boys and their wives are driving in to attend." From talking to this woman, I sense that her enthusiasm for this new endeavor has helped her family to view her in a different light.

I know women who are reading books and taking courses on everything from cooking to bookkeeping. They are continually seeking ways to improve themselves. The improvements not only do wonders for their confidence, but enrich their husbands' and children's lives as well.

Some women think it's acceptable to sacrifice their own growth for their family's sake. What they don't realize is that their growth excites the whole family and gives its members permission to grow, too. Never turn down an opportunity to grow.

chapter 14

A WOMAN'S INTUITION

WHEN I was a single working mother, I struggled to support my family, just as many men were doing at the time. In terms of my earnings, the fact that I had as many bills to pay as my male coworkers is not the point. What should really have mattered to my employer was how well I did my job.

Yet I was paid less than my male peers. It seemed as though I would have to be twice as good as they were to receive equal pay. I was especially troubled when the ideas I presented to my employer were met with, "There you go, Mary Kay, thinking like a woman again!"

In those days, "thinking like a woman" meant you didn't have your head on straight. If women wanted to succeed in the working world, they were expected to be carbon copies of men. It may sound unbelievable now, but many women went along with that precept. You can call it brainwashing, but many of us blindly accepted our place as second-class citizens and believed this nonsense—for a while.

Women *do* think differently from the way men think, but the differences have nothing to do with being inferior to or incompatible with how men think. On the contrary, thinking like a woman can be a tremendous advantage.

Let's begin by acknowledging that we don't always think exactly as men do. Once again, these differences are not necessarily negative, nor should they cause us to be at odds with the opposite sex.

One difference springs from a special quality we possess: our intuitiveness. Admittedly, I have trouble defining "woman's intuition," but I know it exists. Throughout my life, I have witnessed countless situations in which a woman's intuitive response defied logic but turned out to be correct. Perhaps a woman will form an immediate opinion of someone, and no matter how much others reason with her, she refuses to change her mind. Later, when the facts are known—whether she felt instant rapport or a flash of distrust—her first reaction turns out to be right.

Today, Mary Kay Cosmetics has a highly sophisticated marketing research department to guide us in such areas as product development and long-term strategies. But in the beginning, my intuition was my only guide. I didn't conduct marketing surveys to find out what other women thought of the cosmetics they bought over the counter at their local department stores. I didn't have the money for such research. But I did know I felt embarrassed to try on makeup in a store in front of other shoppers. And when I did, no one bothered to teach me how to apply it myself. Sure, the store cosmeticians could make you look like Elizabeth Taylor, but once they were finished, you had no earthly idea what they had done or how to repeat it.

The more I thought about it, the more I thought it would be wonderful for a skin care expert to come to my house and, in the privacy of my home, show me what would be the best look for my face. Then, if she instructed me on how to do it myself, I would be able to do it tomorrow and every day. I believed other women would feel this way, too. Based on that belief, I decided to conduct skin care classes. Right from the start, instinct told me a woman wouldn't mind experimenting with makeup when she was with a few close girlfriends. How did I know they would feel that way? Because that's the way I felt about it.

Shortly thereafter, both my attorney and my accountant told me my original marketing plan was doomed. Normally, when I engage the services of professionals with expertise, I obediently follow their instructions. After all, I'm paying for their advice; if I knew more than they did about their fields, I'd have no reason to seek their counsel. But when something inside gives me different counsel, and I have a strong hunch I'm right, I follow my intuition.

I can't explain it analytically, but when the feeling is deep inside me, I *know* the right thing to do. I've talked about this sense with many women who say that although they can't explain it either, they've learned to trust it.

GOING WITH YOUR SIXTH SENSE

Each time we see, hear, touch, smell, or taste something, that sense sends a message to the brain, and we react in some way. Similarly, we should respond to our sixth sense, woman's intuition, when it sends us a signal.

Unfortunately, we don't always have the same degree of confidence in our intuitive power that we have in our everyday senses. Intuition can be harder to identify. Its ambiguous nature requires us to make a judgment call. Most women experience the five other senses in much the same way, but when it comes to a woman's intuition, hers, yours, and mine may differ. There's no rhyme or reason to how or why we have it. We can't even predict when this intuitive sense will come into play. It just happens, and we can't turn it on and off at will. Despite its evasive nature, when our intuition sends a message, past experience tells us to heed it.

Lane Nemeth, the founder and CEO of Discovery Toys, is a successful executive who allows her woman's intuition to govern many important business decisions. Lane explains that when a decision must be made on a particular toy for the company's product line, she goes with her inner feeling. "Every now and then, I get kind of a chill inside," she says, "and then my body gets goose bumps. When I'm on the fence about what to do and this happens, I think to myself, 'That's it! This is what we're going to do!' and I know it's the right decision."

Whether your intuition expresses itself in goose bumps, a sudden visualization, or just a knowing lift of the eyebrow, after this sense has tipped you off enough times, you learn to trust it.

Sometimes a strategy seems to make no business sense, but just the same, you are convinced your idea is more than just a wild notion. Also, you may get an unexplainable feeling about someone, a feeling that makes sense only to you. Many times, a Mary Kay consultant senses that a woman is interested in our skin care products or marketing plan though she outwardly appears resistant and even makes negative comments. Likewise, a woman in a skin care class can sense when her consultant is truly interested in benefiting her; this customer can also tell when another salesperson is interested only in a commission. When you're shopping for a dress, you usually know whether the salesclerk's compliments are sincere.

Once in a while, when a person has come into my office for a routine matter, out of the clear blue sky I'll feel compelled to ask, "Is there something you'd like to tell me?" I've seen men and women burst into tears when I ask this question and proceed to confide in me about serious illnesses in the family, bad marriages, or other difficulties they're facing.

Besides signaling when something is wrong, woman's intuition covers broad territory. For example, a woman may perceive good in a person, good that has gone unnoticed by others. One of our directors, Lisa Madson, sensed potential in a particular recruit—potential that others might not have perceived. "I never saw such a long résumé," Lisa explains, "She had thirty jobs before joining us, never holding a job more than a few months. But I had a strong feeling that she had just never worked at a job that she really enjoyed. Observing her enthusiasm, I knew she'd be happy in our business. Well, that was six years ago; today, she's a pink Cadillac director."

In 1976, National Sales Director Shirley Hutton flew from Minneapolis to Sioux City in order to recruit Marlys Skillings, whom she had met only through a brief telephone conversation. After that one chat, Shirley bought her plane ticket. In Sioux City, Shirley conducted a skin care class with Marlys present, and following a personal interview, Marlys became a consultant. Shirley's hunch paid off. Marlys has become a national sales director and has so far earned more than two million dollars in her Mary Kay career.

National Sales Director Anne Newbury is a shining example of a woman who uses her intuitive power to build her sales organization. She has recruited several dozen women based on her uncannily accurate first impressions. "On a flight out of Boston," Anne begins one story, "I observed a bubbly flight attendant who had wonderful people skills with passengers. I had an hour layover, so as I disembarked, I introduced myself and said I'd like to chat with her about a wonderful business opportunity for her. 'Do you have a few minutes to talk with me in the terminal?' She consented to meet with me. Sure enough, after our brief conversation, the flight attendant agreed that during her next visit to Boston she would meet with me at length. After spending the afternoon with me in Boston, she became a beauty consultant."

Anne says she has had similar brief encounters with waitresses, salesclerks, and "just about anyone who gives me this kind of feeling that she has something special. Now, how can I tell who has what it takes? I look for a certain glow. That's a characteristic that can't be quantified, but when I get this feeling about a person, I just know she has tremendous potential to succeed in our business."

Senior Sales Director Shirley Oppenheimer also acts on intuition, sometimes getting in her car and driving for several hours to visit a potential beauty consultant. "My husband used to say, 'I can't believe you're going that far for an interview,'" Shirley says. "He knows better now."

"In my heart I could sometimes feel when a particular woman really needed what we had to offer, and I *knew* she'd come into the business after I had the opportunity to meet with her."

Sandy Miller, a national sales director in Munster, Indiana, tells the story of a consultant whom she had recruited twelve years ago and who had moved to Northern California. "For years, Carol had only been a mediocre performer," Sandy says. "She was content with keeping her business at a low level. But a year ago, her husband passed away while waiting for a heart transplant. Carol decided it was time to concentrate on her Mary Kay career. 'I'm ready to do it,' she told me. 'Will you help me?'

"'Of course,' I replied. A few days later, I flew to California to coach her. Now, years before, I had made a few trips to see her, spending a lot of money for which I received little in return. So, as you can see, her track record was not very good. But this time, I felt Carol was ready and I was willing to put in fresh effort. This trip made those other visits worthwhile. Even though everyone told me I was crazy to throw good money after bad, my intuition told me to do it. Sure, sound business logic would have suggested I say, 'First, Carol, show me you're really serious, and after you prove to me during the next three months that you can do this, I'll come out there.'

"Instead, I allowed my intuition to guide me. Once I showed Carol I believed in her, she didn't want to let me down. Ten months later, she became a director and proved me right."

Jan Harris is another national sales director who relies on her intuition when she recruits. "During an interview," she explains, "I am able to sense when a woman has a need in her life, and I show her how a Mary Kay career can fill that need. It may be a financial solution, a sense of camaraderie, or just some fun in her life that we provide. How I sense this in women, I'm not sure. But when I trust those instincts, my batting average is very high."

Over the course of my career, I have worked with thousands and thousands of women. An objective observer would have predicted failure for a number of those who ended up succeeding. Relying on their instincts, they saw a path where no path had been charted, and they had the faith to take it. I enjoy hearing of other women's reliance on intuition to make decisions; their stories reaffirm my belief in this sixth sense that has helped me so much throughout my career.

THE PINK PHENOMENON

Referring to our use of the color pink, a reporter recently commented, "You really had an eye for marketing when you started your company, Mary Kay." I smiled to hear that

197

because, back in 1963, I had no idea that choosing pink had anything to do with being a good marketer. I just knew that practically every home in the United States at the time had a white bathroom. Everything was white—white tile, white towels, white everything. And then as now, most people kept their hair-spray cans, deodorants, and other toiletries on the countertops. Especially then, merchandise sold in drugstores and groceries was designed in bold, bright colors to attract shoppers as they pushed their carts hurriedly down the aisles. While those colors might make merchandise jump off the shelves and into the carts, they ruined the way a bathroom looked, so I used to keep everything hidden away. This led me to think that we should package our products in attractive containers, nice enough for a woman to display on the countertop. After considering numerous colors for our packaging, I decided a soft, delicate pink and gold would look lovely in those white-tile bathrooms.

Contrary to rumor, I didn't pick pink because it was my favorite color. It's not. A group of California psychologists now says the color pink helps soothe overexcited people, but I have to confess, I wasn't interested in pink's tranquilizing effect.

At the time, it never occurred to me that pink could someday become synonymous with Mary Kay products. Yet it has become our trademark. Every time a pink Cadillac goes by, people automatically think, "Mary Kay!"

It was not extensive market surveys or demographic studies that created the pink Cadillac, just pure and simple woman's intuition.

In the autumn of 1968, five years after we started our company, I began shopping for a new car. Business was good, so I decided to buy a new Cadillac. After the salesman went over the options and the price, he asked, "What color do you want, ma'am?"

From my purse I took out our company's lip and eye palette. Like much of our product line, it was pale pink. "This color," I said, handing the palette to him.

The salesman simply laughed, saying, "Oh, no, you don't. Believe me, you don't!"

"Oh, yes, I do!"

"When that car gets here, you are not going to like it!" he exclaimed. "Let me tell you how much it will cost you to have it repainted."

"I want it pink," I assured him. "Please paint it pink."

"Well, all right. But remember, I warned you."

When the car was ready to be picked up, I drove Mel's black Lincoln to the dealership. Traffic was heavy that morning, and whenever I reached an intersection, it seemed like I had to wait forever to get through. On the way home, in my new pink Cadillac, I was amazed at the respect other drivers showed. As I approached each intersection, everyone noticed my car, and many people waved me through. They smiled and nodded approvingly; some gave me a thumbs-up and motioned me to go ahead of them.

When I arrived at the office late that morning in my pink Cadillac, a series of meetings happened to be letting out. When our people saw my car, they had a fit over it! "What do we have to do to get one of those?" they asked.

I wasn't expecting such a reaction. "Well, I don't know," I answered. "Let me take it to Richard and let him put a pencil to this. Maybe he can come up with some numbers on how you can drive a pink Cadillac, too."

Richard calculated a sales figure that a person would have to achieve to earn the use of a pink Cadillac, and some folks thought the requirements were too strict. Yet five brand-new pink Cadillacs were awarded to our top producers in 1969. In 1970, ten were awarded, and twenty pink Cadillacs were awarded to the top twenty producers in 1972. The following year, Richard devised a formula enabling everyone with a certain amount of sales production to earn the use of one.

Currently, there are over $115 million worth of Mary Kay cars on the road. Smaller pink cars are awarded to women at earlier levels of sales production than the pink Cadillac winners have reached. In other countries, we award whatever car citizens consider the epitome of excellence. For example, in Germany, we award pink Mercedes and, in Taiwan, top-of-the-line pink Toyotas. But here in the United States, pink Cadillacs have become part of Americana. Because we give General Motors such a large annual order, their Detroit world headquarters calls our color "Mary Kay Pink."

It all started when I bought that 1968 Cadillac. Did I have any idea that it would someday become a mobile trademark? Not in a million years!

CINDERELLA GIFTS

Several years ago, I was invited to a multibillion-dollar corporation's sales convention in Acapulco. I noticed several of the salesmen wearing green sports jackets. I could tell the coats were brand-new because many of the men's sleeves were too long or too short, or their jackets simply needed some tailoring.

"What are all these green jackets for?" I asked one of the company's vice presidents.

"This year's top salesmen received the jackets as a gift."

"When was the ceremony when the jackets were awarded?" I asked.

"Oh, there was no ceremony," he explained. "The jackets were just sent to their rooms."

That evening, at the convention's main banquet, I eagerly waited for the big moment when the company would recognize its top salesmen. Finally, at the end of the meal, hundreds of balloons fell from the ceiling, and I thought, "Oh, good opening. Now the awards are going to be presented." But much to my surprise, the evening ended there. Not a mention of achievement was made. No applause, no recognition, nothing!

As a guest, I couldn't say anything, but I thought, "This company missed a golden opportunity to proudly award the jackets to their star performers in the presence of their peers!" I was certain the salespeople would have valued the recognition much more than the actual green jackets.

I know some male executives understand the value of recognition, but far too many do not. I just chalk the difference up to woman's intuition.

I'm reminded of one of the first sales contests I entered. The awards were not announced ahead of time, but I worked very hard to win one. Then, my sales manager, who was an avid fisherman, presented me with the prize I had labored to win: a flounder light. I had no idea what it was. Later on, somebody told me it was used to gig fish when you waded into the water wearing hip boots. I was proud of winning the contest, but a flounder light would have been at the bottom of my preferred prize list.

The desire for recognition is a powerful motivator. Anyone who has attended a Mary Kay Seminar knows we recognize our people's achievements with beautiful gifts and tons of verbal appreciation. Exciting prizes are significant symbols of esteem; I believe both words and things are important.

You already know about the pink Cadillacs. Today they are called "trophies on wheels." In 1968, we started awarding diamond rings and diamond bumblebees to our top performers. Of course, as a woman, I knew when I chose this award that there is something about a diamond that appeals to every female. In addition to a diamond's beauty and sparkle, it holds its value. And diamonds last forever.

Based on my intuition, I felt our consultants would react favorably to receiving diamonds. So I asked Richard to meet with the most successful jewelry wholesaler in Dallas. A very nervous Richard placed what was to be the first of many diamond orders with the jeweler—150 diamond rings for $50 apiece. They weren't for our big Seminar, just for a monthly sales contest, so we were worried. If we had only a few winners, we'd be stuck with a drawerful of diamond rings. To promote the contest, we had beautiful full-color brochures printed up, and the rings looked exquisite. Our consultants were so excited, they broke all existing sales records. That year, we ended up buying 659 of those diamond rings. Diamonds indeed motivate women, and we've used them as an incentive ever since.

Besides all the magnificent diamond rings, bracelets, and necklaces we award, perhaps the most coveted prize is a diamond pin in the shape of a bumblebee.

Within our organization, the bumblebee is the ultimate symbol of achievement. The story behind the award is what makes it so meaningful. You see, years ago, aerodynamics engineers studied this amazing insect and concluded it simply *could not fly.* Its wings were too weak and its body too heavy for flight. The study showed that the bumblebee could not be airborne. The word got out and everybody knew this—but they forgot to tell the bumblebee, and he went right on flying! My intuition told me the bumblebee was a perfect symbol for women who have flown to the top.

Our diamond bumblebee is more than a handsome piece of jewelry; it's a badge of merit. Whenever you see anyone wearing one at a Mary Kay function, you know she's a distinguished person in our sales organization. We award four types of bumble-bees. A small bee consists of twenty-one stones—nineteen diamonds set with two emerald eyes; it weighs .75 carats. A larger bee has nineteen diamonds; its eyes can be set with two diamonds or emeralds. It weighs 1.10 carats. The third bee has twenty-one diamonds and weighs 1.75 carats. Finally, we present a special 3.5-carat diamond bee as a gift to our retiring national sales directors.

A long time ago, I realized women would especially appreciate exotic presents—items they would never buy them for themselves. Hence we give such awards as diamonds, pink Cadillacs, and trips to faraway places.

I call them "Cinderella gifts" because the typical woman is too practical to buy one of these luxuries for herself. I know some companies offer cash bonuses as incentives, but I don't think money has the same heartfelt effect on women. If we awarded a cash bonus, a woman would probably use it to pay her utility bills, make a house payment, or replace her washing machine. Once she spends the money, she doesn't think about it again. But every time she sees that diamond ring on her finger, she remembers her well-deserved moment of glory.

While exotic gifts are wonderful motivational tools, they are also expensive, so a company can't give them to everyone. But inexpensive gifts work wonders, too. In addition to awarding millions of colorful ribbons, we've presented all kinds of pins, costume jewelry, and goblets. Yes, goblets! There's a special story behind what is known as our Golden Goblet Club. We had been in business a few years when I wanted to run a contest that would award a beautiful gold-plated goblet as an award for each monthly wholesale production of one thousand dollars. When a consultant had earned a set of twelve, she would win a matching tray. When she had earned twenty, she'd receive a pitcher, completing the set for her dining room.

When I excitedly explained my idea to Richard, he looked at me in disbelief. "We're dealing with reality," he told me. "At this time, our top producers sell approximately $150 a week, and you're talking $1,000 a month. Do you think they're going to work that much harder—for *that cup?*"

"Yes, Richard," I replied, "they will work to win a golden goblet. We will make it a very exclusive club, which means only a few select women will ever get one, let alone the entire set. They'll work hard to get it because they want the recognition that goes along with it."

"I think you've lost your mind," he answered, "but if you think it will work, we'll do it."

Even I was surprised at how hard the women worked to surpass their own sales records and win those goblets. Two years later, we were giving away so many, we had to stop inscribing them. A few years after that, a number of consultants and directors had such a collection, they began asking if we would like to buy some of the goblets back.

Of course, you don't have to be a Mary Kay beauty consultant to receive a Cinderella gift. If your company doesn't provide incentives that motivate you, why not accomplish the same thing on your own? For instance, I know an interior decorator who rewards herself with a piece of jewelry or a new outfit when she accomplishes a difficult task. And when an independent insurance broker I know exceeds a self-imposed weekly sales quota, she treats herself to a pair of earrings or takes her boyfriend out for a gourmet meal. A weekend away with her family is the way one real estate broker marks the closing of a big sale. So whether you purchase a silk blouse, rent a video on the way home, or just turn off the phone for an hour to curl up with a good book, you can reward yourself for a stellar performance. A bit of advice: Don't apply your self-bestowed "bonus" to the mortgage or a new washing machine—those aren't Cinderella gifts!

WOMEN WHO THINK LIKE MEN

As our company has grown, we have worked hard to keep that fresh, sincere thinking we had when we began. We want to maintain our beliefs and principles, and, equally important, we want to keep the creative juices flowing. Sometimes, when small businesses grow into big businesses, they become buried in bureaucracy—decisions are made by committees, suggestions must be reviewed by ever-higher levels of management, and, as a result, ideas get lost in an involuntary administrative shuffle.

Sometimes women bogged down in such bureaucracies become so involved in their corporate lives, they stop thinking as they always have. In their efforts to compete with men, they start thinking like men. This is unfortunate because they then fail to capitalize on one of their most valuable assets—their woman's intuition. Many women caught up in man's competitive, dog-eat-dog world become harsh, overbearing, and uncaring. They may not even realize their natural intuitive power is slipping away.

Women are blessed with a sixth sense. We must appreciate this remarkable gift and use it to soar to the highest heights.

chapter 15

DOING WELL
BY DOING GOOD

To ENSURE that our company treats all women equally, we have our "ladder of success." Every member of our sales organization knows exactly what she has to do to reach the top. It doesn't matter if the boss doesn't like the way she parts her hair. Nor does race, religion, age, limited education, or any other factor restrain anyone's opportunity to climb the Mary Kay ladder of success. Our company was founded on this premise, and we abide by it as much today as we did when our doors opened in 1963.

While the desire to provide opportunities for women is admirable, it's not enough by itself to start a business. A product that fills a need of consumers is critical. I had three reasons for selecting skin care products. First, I wanted a product that would fill a void in the marketplace by benefiting the women who used it. Yes, many other cosmetics companies were operating then, but none emphasized skin care. It was obvious to me that a woman must have good skin under those cosmetics to have a truly pretty face.

My second reason for choosing skin care products was that a woman must be able to believe in the product she is selling.

After she has tried our products and knows they are good, she can happily recommend them to others.

I knew from my past experience in direct sales that I needed to choose a product that generates repeat orders. This was my third reason for selecting skin care products. A woman who is convinced they're good for her skin will buy more when her supply runs out. Treated right, she could become a lifelong customer. I believed winning loyal customers was essential because in the direct sales field, little is spent on advertising. Rather than putting money into expensive magazine ads or TV commercials, we pass that money on to our sales organization. And the enthusiasm of a beauty consultant carries over to her customer.

THE JOY OF GIVING

As I explained earlier, our company was founded on two fundamental philosophies. One centers around the Golden Rule, and the other focuses on running our lives according to the proper priorities.

From time to time, a critic will scrutinize our company and decide that our philosophies are too simplistic. The critic will declare that a business based on the Golden Rule lacks sophistication. Nonetheless, we have adhered to these philosophies, which are now deeply embedded in all facets of our company. We base every important business decision at Mary Kay Cosmetics on these beliefs.

During every consultant's initial orientation, she learns our basic principles. "Your role is to give," we tell her. You'll find this perspective throughout our organization. A director needs to focus not on commissions but on how she can help a consultant reach within herself to bring out talents she never realized were there. Based on the idea that it is better to give than to receive, each member of our sales organization has been assigned a mission: to serve others.

We give keepsakes to everyone who attends our Seminars, and several years ago, every woman received a pin of two small gold-plated shovels. One shovel was larger than the other. The two shovels symbolized that all you send into the lives of others comes back into your own. When you give to others with your little shovel, God gives back to you with his big shovel. We assiduously communicate this message to our sales organization: Do your kind deeds without expecting anything in return, and over the course of time, good will come back to you.

The women who ultimately succeed in our company are those who truly believe this. One such person is Harriet Pennick, who was a practicing pediatrician when she joined Mary Kay Cosmetics in 1988. She was introduced to the company when her nurse, Betty Neal, a Mary Kay director, invited her to a guest event. "The first year, I only piddled at Mary Kay," Harriet says. But the stress of pediatrics began to work on her: "Doctors get their highs from other people's lows; bringing back a child from the jaws of death is a very stressful way to get a rush. I came into Mary Kay to get that warm feeling." Over a period of time, Harriet realized that Mary Kay made her happier than medicine, giving her more lasting comfort.

As a physician, Harriet spent her time taking care of children's medical needs. Now that she is devoting herself to a new career, she says, "As a Mary Kay director, I can stroke a woman until she feels better about herself, until she looks as good as she feels, and until her self-esteem can be raised to where it should be. I do this always in hopes that her children's lives will be better than ever before. And in that sense, at least indirectly, I feel that I am still helping those children for whom I went to medical school."

Giving is one of life's greatest joys. Those who are able to experience this joy daily—and get paid for it—are indeed fortunate. Regrettably, not every career offers this particular reward. Millions of people go to jobs every day where they cannot reach out and touch people. Although clerks and factory workers, for instance, receive various satisfactions from their careers, they may have no direct contact with the consumer. Consequently, they miss the joy of giving. If your career does not provide this pleasure, don't despair. You can contribute to the well-being of people in many other ways. Volunteer your time. Homeless shelters, hospitals, and churches are a few of the places waiting for your special touch. One elderly lady I know spends several hours a week reading to a man who has lost his sight. Another friend tutors inner-city children after school. There's a long list of wonderful causes that you can make your own. Reach out and help somebody.

DOING THE RIGHT THING

Some time ago, I read an article about Robert Haas, great-great-grandnephew of the Levi Strauss who founded the giant apparel company in the early 1840s. When Robert Haas was named CEO of Levi Strauss & Co. in 1984, he wondered how he could manage the business without sacrificing the Golden Rule philosophy that had been ingrained in the company from the start. Haas recalled that the company had paid all of its employees during the time following the San Francisco earthquake of 1906 when the company had to rebuild its original factory. Even through the Great Depression, when the company suffered hard times, it had not laid off a single employee.

Haas also thought about an event that took place in the early 1960s, prior to the passing of the Civil Rights Act of 1964. Levi Strauss acquired a factory in Blackstone, Virginia, where blacks and whites were segregated. When Levi Strauss announced intentions to integrate operations, many of the white employees and townspeople resisted the idea. After much debate, the white workers consented to most of their new employer's demands, but still insisted on separate rest rooms. "No deal," said the plant manager. Then the resisters proposed putting an aisle down the middle of the plant floor, with blacks on one side, whites on the other. Standing on principle, Levi Strauss again rejected their offer. In the end, the Blackstone factory was fully integrated.

Since Haas took control more than ten years ago, he has upheld the high principles his predecessors established long before he was born. With the same conviction possessed by his great-great-granduncle, Robert Haas explains, "A company's values are crucial to its competitive success. You can't say one thing and be another. People detect fakes unerringly. Your employees won't put into practice values that you're not practicing."

A woman whose heart is in the right place is Gun Denhart, cofounder and CEO of Hanna Andersson. Following the birth of her son, Christian, in 1980, she and her husband, Tom, dreamed up a business that would sell one-hundred-percent cotton baby clothes—the kind that had the comfortable softness and high quality she had known growing up in Sweden. "Everything out there was polyester," Gun explains. "The baby clothes were not soft to the hand, and they lasted only a few washings. I wanted to produce clothing like what the children wear in Sweden."

In the summer of 1983, the Denharts contacted a Swedish garment firm to manufacture their first line of goods, and the family moved from New York City to Portland, Oregon, to set up shop. By February 1984, the first Hanna Andersson catalog was out. (The company is named for Gun's grandmother.)

I am impressed with the high quality of Hanna Andersson merchandise because the soft clothes wear so well. But I am even more impressed with how the company stands behind its products. During its first year in business, Hanna Andersson established Hannadowns, an innovative program that encourages customers to return their "Hannas" after their children have outgrown them. These clothes are then donated to needy children, and the customer receives a credit of 20 percent of the original purchase price. As a consequence, thousands of children have received Hannadowns. While doing good for others, Hanna Andersson has prospered. Sales for 1993, ten years after the business was founded, exceeded forty-four million dollars. The company has distributed more than 240,000 items of clothing to charities and crisis centers, and it currently donates about 4,000 items per month.

Another entrepreneur who does well by doing good is Mo Siegel, who founded Celestial Seasonings in 1971. Just out of his teens, Mo started the company that has become a household name to drinkers of herbal tea. Today, his unique packaging is practically as well-known as the product itself. But Mo flatly denies that the decorative boxes displaying philosophic messages were designed as a marketing tool. "The space is there, so why not use it to do some good?" he asserts. "If it can be used to enrich other people's lives, then I say, 'By all means, do so.' Besides, it's better this way than to use it for advertising. People have advertising crammed down their throats all the time. If our package can give them something about life— something interesting or something funny—then let's do it. But let's give them something that adds human value."

Words of wisdom appear on the sides, bottom, and inside flaps of each Celestial Seasonings tea box. For instance, on one box, a Confucian saying reads, "The man who in the view of gain thinks of righteousness; who in the view of danger is prepared to give up his life; and who does not forget an old agreement however far back it extends—such a man may be reckoned a complete man." Another of my favorites reads simply, "The most important thing a father can do for his children is to love their mother."

Mo says his sole motivation for presenting these messages is to relay meaningful thoughts to others. He explains, "When I've died and I'm resurrected on the day of judgment, I imagine the Ancient of Days pulling out the record book and asking me, 'Mo, what did you do with your life?'

"Then I answer, 'Well, I sold more herb tea than anyone in the world.'

" 'Yes. But what did you do with your life that's of value?'

" 'I cornered the soybean market; it was incredible. I made so much money.'

" 'But, Mo, *what did you do of value with your life?*' "

Mo continues, "I think of that at least once a week. I want to make sure that when the record book is opened, I can say, 'I raised a good family. I put out products that were nutritionally good for people. I felt like I was serving people.' "

In the world today, so many businesspeople are doing well by doing good. Robert Haas, Gun Denhart, and Mo Siegel are only a few examples.

AND THEN SOME

A very successful businessman was once asked, "To what do you attribute your success?"

213

"I can tell you in three words," he answered. *"And then some."*

"What do you mean, 'and then some'?" he was questioned.

"Do everything that's expected of you," he explained, "and then some."

Isn't this a beautiful philosophy for living? We should give so much of ourselves—and then some! Imagine how wonderful the world would be if everyone lived by this philosophy.

I heard a lovely story about a woman in San Francisco who, upon driving up to a tollbooth at the Golden Gate Bridge, handed the operator seven tokens and said, "Would you please tell the six drivers behind me that the car ahead paid their way?" Imagine the surprise and pleasure those six people felt when they heard the news. I'm sure it gave them a warm feeling that lasted the entire day. In fact, they probably felt so good, they couldn't wait to do a good deed for somebody else.

Since hearing this story, I have suggested to every member of our sales force that she perform a random act of kindness for someone every day: "Do something unexpected—something that nobody could have predicted." If all Mary Kay salespeople did this on a routine basis, in only a short time their acts would total millions of good deeds. And if others responded by doing still more good deeds, this goodness could touch practically every man, woman, and child in America!

At our Seminars, one of the most esteemed forms of recognition is our Go-Give Award, which is presented to an individual who exemplifies the true spirit of giving to others. The award serves as a memorial to Sue Z. Vickers, a national sales director who was murdered in 1978 after being kidnapped from a Dallas shopping center. Sue will always be remembered for her beauty and loving personality, and the Go-Give Award is an ongoing remembrance of her generous nature. It affirms to every member of our sales organization that the company places value on doing good for others.

Our entire business, in fact, is based on giving to others, yet this openhandedness extends beyond the world of Mary Kay Cosmetics. Giving has no boundaries. Let me tell you about a rewarding experience I had in the late 1960s. One Saturday afternoon, I accompanied a friend to the Green Stamp redemption center. Although I had accumulated a large stack of Green Stamp books, I was frustrated because I couldn't find anything I needed. Later that same day, I read a story in the newspaper about a small church that was trying to raise money to purchase a van for transporting children to and from its religious school. "So that's why I didn't spend my stamps today!" I said to myself.

On Sunday morning, I got up half an hour early so I could stop by the Tabernacle Baptist Church on the way to my own church service. I felt somewhat self-conscious driving my pink Cadillac through a poor section of town, and I was even apprehensive about stopping to ask for directions when I couldn't find the church. Finally, I spotted a small building I had driven past several times, thinking it was a house. Even though there was no sign, I realized it was the Tabernacle Baptist Church.

I went inside and asked for the Reverend Moses Reagan. He wasn't available, but Mrs. Reagan was. When she walked into the room to greet me, she spotted those stamp books in my hand. "Oh, thank the Lord for you!" she said. She insisted on showing me around, and during my short tour, Mrs. Reagan explained that during the week, the church served as a day nursery, but on Sunday, it was used for services. On the Sabbath, the children assembled in a small room to attend Sunday school classes.

My visit was interrupted by a phone call. After taking the call, Mrs. Reagan said to me, "Oh, what am I going to do? That was our beginner Sunday-school teacher calling in sick."

"Well, I taught beginners in Sunday school for twenty years," I said. "Perhaps I can help."

Mrs. Reagan agreed to have me conduct the class and told me the children usually heard a Bible story. So that Sunday, I skipped the service at my church and taught Sunday school at the Tabernacle Baptist Church.

I happened to be the only white person in the church that morning, and I was dressed in a white angora outfit. The children couldn't stop staring at me.

Evidently Mrs. Reagan thought I did a good job, because she invited me back for the following Sunday. To make a long story short, I taught Sunday school there for two years. Pretty soon, I started bringing the children cookies and snacks and, later, little gifts. Because I had worn that white dress on the first day, the children referred to me as their white angel. Although I eventually returned to my own church, over the years Mary Kay Cosmetics has supported Tabernacle Baptist with prayers and donations. The church got stamp books *and then some,* but I got even more for helping them.

MAKING A DIFFERENCE

With six billion human beings inhabiting our planet, individuals sometimes feel insignificant and doubt that one person can really make a difference in this world. Well, believe me, *one person can.* It is important to remember that you do not have to change a certain number of lives. By reaching out to just one person, you can make a difference. That person can be anyone—a child, a friend, a customer, a homeless person, anyone at all.

We make a difference in many ways. We do it when we perform a random act of kindness for a stranger or a series of and-then-somes for a loved one; the list is endless. You don't have to win the Nobel Peace Prize, find a cure for cancer, or alter the course of civilization. Making a difference requires only your willingness to give to others—the more often the better.

What's interesting about subscribing to a life of giving is that you become addicted. It's a good addiction. Once you get into the habit of reaching out to others, you somehow always want to do more. When we opened Mary Kay Cosmetics, my biggest ambition was to provide wonderful opportunities for women in the Dallas area. At the time, I had no idea we'd someday be able to make opportunities available to women not only outside of Dallas, but outside of Texas, and even outside of the United States. We are currently offering the Mary Kay opportunity to women in twenty-three countries. We entered the Russian market in late 1993, and Mary Kay Cosmetics is now in business in mainland China. There was a time when I would have thought it ludicrous to say this, but now I can honestly declare that I won't be satisfied until every woman in the world has an opportunity to be a Mary Kay consultant and live the Mary Kay way of life.

As we enter two of the world's biggest markets, Russia and China, our initial accomplishments will be realized by two special women. I've already told you about one of them, Julie Rasmussen, who is heading our company in Russia. Another bright young star on our horizon is Cecilia Yang, who will play an instrumental role in our expansion into China. Born

217

and raised in Taiwan, where she majored in journalism at school, Cecilia came to the United States as a graduate student and earned her MBA at Dartmouth College's business school, Amos Tuck. Upon graduating in 1991, Cecilia was hired by Bausch & Lomb, where she eventually worked her way up to the position of marketing director in the Asia/Pacific Division.

"A recruiter was playing golf with a friend of mine," Cecilia explains, "and mentioned he was looking for 'a Chinese Mary Kay.' My friend suggested that he contact me for the position. I already knew a lot about Mary Kay Cosmetics, so I said I'd be interested in being considered for the position of introducing the company to the mainland.

"After meeting with the recruiter, I became fascinated with the idea of making Mary Kay products available to Chinese women. With China's population of one billion people, I kept thinking about all those women who, due to the political situation, have been deprived of looking beautiful like women in the Western world. I know these women desperately want to have a better life. They have seen what the women in Taiwan and Hong Kong have, and they want it, too.

"To be able to go to China and help make the women there look beautiful is my mission in life. I already know they'll be beautiful on the outside once we show them how to apply their makeup. I am equally challenged to provide Chinese women with an opportunity to feel beautiful inside because, with the independence we bring them, they'll have renewed self-esteem."

When Cecilia notified Bausch & Lomb of her decision to join Mary Kay Cosmetics, the company tried to induce her to stay by offering her a high-ranking marketing position in the Asia/Pacific Division at the same pay we had committed to her. She refused, explaining, "You offer me a fine job, but Mary Kay Cosmetics is offering me a lifetime opportunity of helping my Chinese sisters.

"What appeals to me most about Mary Kay is providing an opportunity to Chinese women to go into business for themselves, but not by themselves," Cecilia says. "These women will work hard, but they need us to train and work with them to make their business happen. The Chinese women are accustomed to being taught and trained, but they live in a country that hasn't allowed them to have any business experience. The Mary Kay philosophy of helping women to help themselves will be a perfect fit for Chinese women. I am so excited to be a part of it."

Like Cecilia, Julie Rasmussen has a strong desire to help women in a changing country. Julie states that her work in Russia is not a job but a mission. "This is an incredible period in Russia's history," she explains. "The country is building a new society and, in particular, building a base for capitalism. Mary Kay Cosmetics is participating in that process; we're adding and contributing to it. We are helping families live better. When a mother is happy and earning money, her children eat better, dress better, and enjoy better lives."

Julie is convinced that our company has a great future in Russia because, unlike other cosmetic companies that have begun exporting products there, we offer skin care information and personal service. "We don't just ship a batch of merchandise to Russia, let it run out, and then send another shipment," Julie says. "The most important thing we do is support our Russian consultants, and we will never let them down. By doing this, we are building their trust, and we plan to be there forever."

Cecilia and Julie want to make a difference in the lives of millions of women. By giving women a chance to create financial and psychological independence in countries where such opportunities are rare, these two young women are making this a better world for all of us.

chapter 16

EVERY BUSINESS IS
A PEOPLE BUSINESS

*T*HE GREAT CEO of General Motors, Alfred Sloan, was a business leader who understood that a corporation's greatest resource is its people. Sloan once said, "Take my assets but leave me my organization, and, in five years, I'll have it all back." Sloan understood that every business is a people business.

In the early 1920s, with Sloan at the helm, General Motors began to challenge Ford as the number one automaker. It was Sloan's people skills that pushed GM ahead of Ford, and once the giant automaker had an edge, the company never looked over its shoulder. General Motors went on to become the world's largest industrial company.

People are definitely a company's greatest asset. It doesn't make any difference whether the product is cars or cosmetics. A company is only as good as the people it keeps. And in order to attract and retain good people, a business must treat people right. Without people skills, no organization—and for that matter, no manager—can make it in today's highly competitive business environment.

THE INVISIBLE SIGN

I have learned to imagine an invisible sign around each person's neck that says, "Make me feel important!" Today I see this sign on everyone I meet, and I respond to it immediately. I never cease to be amazed at how positively people react when they're made to feel important.

If I were to teach a first-year management course at the college level, on day one, I'd pass out a make-me-feel-important sign to every student. I would instruct them to wear the signs in class every day for the entire term. Like Pavlov's theory of conditioned response, by the end of the school term and for the rest of their lives, they'd imagine a sign hanging from the neck of everyone they met. Imagine how enlightened these young people would be. What wonderful relationships they would build with their spouses, friends, coworkers, clients, and customers!

When infants cry, we pick them up and they soon stop crying. Mostly, they cry because they want attention—and they want to be loved. Wanting recognition is a natural desire for all people. While our cries for love may not be as obvious, we cry for it all of our lives. In every culture in the world, people crave recognition and acceptance.

National Sales Director Arlene Lenarz is a real pro at making people feel important. "When a woman comes to a unit meeting," she explains, "I welcome her with open arms. She *knows* I'm excited to have her there and that I don't take her attendance for granted. I act as if she is the most important person in the group. No matter how many women are present, I let each of them know I couldn't hold this meeting without her."

Of course, many other organizations show by their actions that they know the value of making people feel important.

Federal Express does it by inscribing the name of an employee's child on the nose of each new airplane it purchases. At General Mills's headquarters, new employees are allowed to choose a work of art for their personal offices from a large collection of paintings. At Sports Topps Manufacturing, employees in the company's snowbelt regions who meet certain goals are rewarded by being invited on dogsled treks. And IBM knows how to make a lasting impression: At a company affair, a suitcase or a small wheelbarrow filled with dollar bills may be dumped on a table as a sales manager invites the recipient, "Please come up here to pick up your money!" Meanwhile, the master of ceremonies praises the top performer by telling the audience what exceptional act has occasioned the award. Recognizing a person in front of his or her peers makes a powerful statement and elevates self-esteem.

Unfortunately, some companies subscribe to a different school of thought. I have run across managers who criticize and berate subordinates in an attempt to motivate them. These managers apparently believe threats and rebukes inspire people to perform at a peak level. The notion that people work better under the pressure of disapproval is a common misconception. But negative criticism results in negative performance. Fear motivation simply does not work!

A young woman who worked as a sporting goods sales representative told me how she was treated by her sales manager. "The company was having a sales contest," Rita explained to me, "and for its grand prize, the names of two retail accounts of the winning sales rep would be listed in a national advertising campaign. A winner from each of four regions would be announced at the end of a three-month period."

"But what would the sales rep receive?" I asked.

"The winners would receive gratitude from those two accounts that they submitted to be placed in the ad," she said.

223

It sounded like a pretty indirect incentive to me, but wait, there was more.

"I received a call from my sales manager at the end of the first month," Rita continued, "and he screamed, 'Rita, you're the worst rep in the entire company. You're so far behind the pack, you've got to work harder, or I may have to let you go.'

"I was really down in the dumps after that first call, and imagine how I felt when he called a month later. 'Have you no self-respect, Rita?' he asked. 'How can your numbers be so bad? What do you do out there?'

"Since I felt I was trying my best, my self-esteem was so low I was ready to quit. However, at the end of the month, I received another call from the sales manager. 'Give me the names of your two top accounts, Rita.'

"'What for?' I asked.

"'It's for the contest,' he grunted.

"'The contest? But I thought I was doing badly.'

"'I don't know how you did it, but you were number one in your region,' he mumbled, 'so I'm putting your two top accounts in the ad.' Then he hung up."

Rita said she was so upset to be told continually how badly she was doing, she submitted her resignation a few weeks after winning the sales contest.

Sigmund Freud emphasized that work, along with love, is one of the essential sources of self-esteem and meaning in life. Knowing this, astute managers challenge their people to perform to their fullest capacity and give them opportunities to advance to key positions. These managers recognize their people's achievements and shower them with praise. Inducing workers to give their best effort is the primary job of every manager. While some managers try to lead by instilling fear, results are far superior when they lead by example and through encouragement. When workers want what management wants, a company can prosper.

The great American philosopher William James said, "The deepest principle of human nature is the craving to be appreciated and the desire to be important." Always remember that invisible sign.

THE PERSONAL TOUCH

I recently participated in a conference held in Dallas at which thirty-seven CEOs from various major corporations were present. All the CEOs were men. When I was introduced, a short film about our company was shown, and in it, I could be seen congratulating four hundred of our employees at a perfect-attendance meeting. The film depicted much applause as each person came to the head table to receive an award—as well as a kiss—from me. All in all, I kissed a lot of people that day, including some big, burly men who work in our manufacturing plant.

Following the visual presentation, I started my speech by saying, "Well, I'm here to tell you about how our company operates and what you can do to incorporate some of our management style into your own operation. But some of what I do just isn't going to have the same impact if you guys do it. For example, I don't think you male CEOs are going to be able to get away with the kissing part you saw in the film."

As I told my audience about our methods and manners, I could tell from the reaction that the way we treat people was foreign to many of them. Many were shocked that everybody in our company calls me by my first name. "When someone calls me Mrs. Ash," I told them, "I say, 'Please, it's Mary Kay.

If you call me Mrs. Ash, I'll think you don't know me or don't like me. Please call me Mary Kay.'

"Often I tell employees, 'I don't want you to think of me as the chairman emeritus. Think of me as your friend.'"

I explained that we try to create a family-like atmosphere in our company. I then invited the CEOs to tour our headquarters when the meeting adjourned. After the tour, they made scores of comments on the friendliness of our people, from the plant floor to the executive suites. In a thank-you note I received from one CEO, he wrote: "I got a warm, fuzzy feeling while visiting your company, Mary Kay. I walked out on a high. That's exactly how I want people to feel when they visit our facilities. It was a real eye-opener to witness the warmness that permeates your company, and, believe me, we're going to work on making it happen in our company."

When visitors go on a tour of our building, their last stop is generally my office. If I'm not in, they enjoy seeing my pink office. When there's no meeting taking place in my office and I'm by myself, I'll go out to the reception area to greet them. I get such surprised looks when I come out to talk to people and shake their hands. They act as though they can't believe a company founder would do that. I want them to leave with a warm feeling about our company, and since it's their last stop, meeting the company's founder should be icing on the cake.

I'm asked why I take the time to meet with these tour groups. "It adds a personal touch," I explain, "and a dimension that one rarely experiences in a big company."

Over the years, large numbers of groups have toured our building. I have found that when twenty women tell twenty other women about the warm feeling they had while visiting our company, and those twenty women tell twenty more, a lot of people are getting positive vibes about Mary Kay Cosmetics. We project an image to the public that we truly care about people—an image that reflects reality. I know ours is not the usual treatment people get at companies, but then, it has never been our intention to be a run-of-the-mill company.

When we were a small, start-up company, we worked very hard to become a big company. Now we're working hard to continue to operate like a small company. In particular, we cherish the personal touch. And as everyone knows, that's an easy quality to lose in a large organization.

An ongoing goal of every company is to sustain growth. A company that stands still really goes backward and is likely to get swallowed up by the competition. Also, a big company can provide certain advantages, including economies of scale and expensive research. It takes a large company to operate a railroad, an airline, an automobile manufacturing plant, or a public utility.

On the other hand, the small business can best provide the personal touch—like the friendly hello you get from the owner of the corner grocery store or the personal service a dress shop owner gives because she knows your size and taste in clothes.

Certainly nobody likes the impersonal feeling of dealing with an insensitive monolithic corporation. For this reason, at Mary Kay Cosmetics, we work very hard to "think small," even while we continue to expand.

It's often the little things that count, and nobody should ever be so big that he or she forgets them. Little things that everyone appreciates include being on time for appointments and returning telephone calls promptly. When you fail to follow through on a seemingly insignificant detail, you send the message, "You're not important enough for me to care about you."

As you know by now, I place a lot of emphasis on tending to details. For instance, every one of our 2,500 staff members receives a card from me congratulating them on their anniversary with the company. I always say something special, such as, "Can you believe we're celebrating your twenty-fifth anniversary? Does time ever fly!" or "How is it possible that this is your thirteenth anniversary? Thank you so much for thirteen wonderful years." Sometimes I just say, "I think you're great!" or "You are wonderful!"

Our organization is so large now, it's no longer possible for me to communicate personally with everyone. However, I make several phone calls every day to people in the field who have accomplished extraordinary things. When a tragedy, such as a diagnosis of cancer, strikes someone, I'll often call to offer a few words of encouragement.

In today's high-tech world, we must strive to make sure an individual doesn't feel like a number being spewed out of a computer. That feeling is the epitome of impersonalization.

An incident of this nature almost occurred recently when I stopped in to say hello at a "New Director Development Week." Many forms of recognition are given at our classes. A person must have thirty recruits just to qualify to attend. Directors who have forty recruits in their unit by the end of their first month as a director earn the right to sit in the front row of the class on a pink pillow. And any new director who has recruited fifty or more consultants receives an autographed pink pillow to take home with her.

As chairman emeritus, I pass out the pink pillows. One by one, the recipient's name is announced, and I make the presentation. This time, at the end of the brief ceremony to award the pillows, I said, "These names are done by computer, and sometimes people and computers can make mistakes. Is there anyone we've missed?" Four hands went up, so I immediately requested four more pink pillows. No questions were asked; I just wanted to make sure these women who had worked hard for this honor were not left out. In my opinion, it would be unforgivable to omit someone who had earned the recognition, even at the risk of giving a pink pillow to someone who had not actually earned it. After all, it's only a pink pillow!

Another way I maintain the personal touch is by never sitting behind my desk when someone visits my office. Instead, if someone settles on the couch, I pull up a chair and sit down beside her. When a small group of people are present, I sit with them in a circle. I do this because I want my guests to feel comfortable. A desk is a barrier. I remember having conversations with former employers as they regally sat behind their desks. Their attitude was "Me boss, you peon." That's not a message I want to convey to anyone.

PEOPLE WILL SUPPORT THAT WHICH THEY HELP TO CREATE

In the 1980s, scores of bestselling books on Japanese management advocated decision making by consensus. It was a time when Japanese products, ranging from automobiles to television sets, were outselling American products, and U.S. managers scrambled to learn new ways to motivate their people.

While decision making by consensus may appear to be a revolutionary new style of management, Mary Kay Cosmetics has followed it since our founding. I've mentioned before that a popular saying around our company is: "People will support that which they help to create." As discussed in chapter 11, even when people are dissatisfied with the status quo, they resist change. People involved in the decision-making process are more likely to accept change and support new ideas. Involving them means soliciting their advice, listening to their comments, and inviting them to participate in implementation. The involvement of large numbers of people does cause some processes to slow down, but this inconvenience is offset by the tremendous benefits of high morale. Additionally, once a change is implemented, the strong support it receives creates high-yield results.

During my days in the field, I observed that beauty consultants who weren't performing up to par tended to skip sales meetings, which only made matters worse. To encourage someone to attend a sales meeting, I would call her and say, "Gee, I missed you at the last sales meeting. I wonder if you would do me a favor for the meeting next week. I need someone to do a ten-minute talk on the subject of doing eye makeup."

Even if she wasn't good at it, I still wanted her to take part in the meeting. She'd have to prepare herself and do some homework in order to talk. Every director, instead of conducting a two-hour meeting by herself, gets other women on her team to participate in their areas of expertise.

Our sales organization has a saying: "If you've had a bad week, you need the meeting. If you've had a good week, the meeting needs you." When everyone participates, it ensures a good meeting. (Did you ever notice that the best sales meeting you ever attended was when you were on the program?)

Every good salesperson understands the concept that "people will support that which they help to create." In auto sales, a prospect often turns into a buyer during the demonstration ride. What gets the customer involved isn't talking about the car, but getting behind the wheel. There is power in moving someone from a passive to an active role. Likewise, a computer salesperson likes to see a shopper at the keyboard moving the mouse around. At skin care classes, our beauty consultants encourage participation by showing each woman how to make up her own face. Salespeople refer to this as "bringing the customer into the act." The more involved you become, the more confident you will be in making a decision.

Anyone can learn a lesson from this sales concept. When children ask their parents for help on homework, guess who ends up doing it! A smart wife will ask her husband for his advice on decorating the house; instead of resisting her, he becomes involved. Perhaps your manager has invited you to participate in some early planning sessions. So why not return the gesture by asking for advice on one of your projects? Chances are, you'll get support as well as ideas.

THE SPEED OF THE LEADER
IS THE SPEED OF THE GANG

When Caesar went into battle, he wore a bright red cape. General Patton revered Caesar, so he painted his tank bright red. Both of these men demonstrated great leadership; they risked their own lives, and inspired their troops to follow them. Caesar and Patton did what leaders are supposed to do: They led.

When a Mary Kay director meeting comes to an impasse, someone is likely to say, "The speed of the leader is the speed of the gang." Everyone there knows exactly what she means. This saying alerts us to lead by example. A good sales director should set the pace for her unit. She knows better than to advise, "Do as I say, not as I do."

One day back in the mid-1970s, a group of our top executives was in my office discussing how to promote the value of conducting two skin care classes a day to our consultants; if they did so, their earnings would substantially increase. Someone came up with the idea that if I held ten skin care classes in one week, it would send a message to every consultant and director that they could, too.

Since I hadn't held ten classes over the last ten years, it was quite a challenge. But I knew my doing ten classes would remove the doubts of any woman who wondered whether she could. "OK, I'll do it," I agreed.

Immediately, panic set in. How was I going to find ten women to host the ten classes? All my friends had already hosted several skin care classes each. If they hadn't hosted a class, then they probably were no longer my friends! I was looking forlornly around the room when I had an idea.

"Phil, you're new with the company. Has your wife Carol ever held a class?"

"Uh, no," he said.

"Fine. You tell Carol I'm going to be calling her. She's going to love this new experience!"

By going around the room, I was able to schedule several more classes. It amazed me that so many consultants and directors had walked past the offices of these executives and never thought to ask them, "Has your wife ever held a Mary Kay skin care class?"

A few trips down the hall later, I had ten classes lined up. I felt good about having accomplished in a brief time what had looked like a Herculean task. And I did it by looking in the most obvious place—around me.

Soon, word of the plan was out, and the sales department promoted it to the hilt. A ten-class contest was set up to see who could hold ten classes on the same week that I was doing ten classes. To ensure I'd get my ten in, I booked four extras in case any had to be canceled. One was a Saturday afternoon skin care class for five men, my husband's stockbroker friends.

Many changes had occurred over the previous ten years, so I did my homework thoroughly. While I had been involved backstage with changes in our product line, I had never practiced the mechanics of actually applying them in a class or using all of the new colors available. I didn't even know how to assemble our new display case.

On the weekend before my big week, the new issue of *Applause* magazine arrived at my house. An article featured my acceptance of the ten-class challenge. Needless to say, knowing that thousands of our people would be watching to see me fulfill my pledge, I felt pressure. I knew consultants would be asking themselves, "Can she really do it?" Others might think, "If Mary Kay can't do it, it can't be done!"

Did I ever practice that weekend! I learned the details of every item, and I read the latest research literature. I reread the sales manual that I had written years ago.

I'll spare you the details of that momentous week. Suffice it to say, I taught exactly ten skin care classes and booked nineteen for the future, which I subsequently turned over to someone else. I also recruited two new consultants, and my sales volume was $2,590. (Remember, this was at a time when a dollar went a lot farther than it does today.) Later, when the top producers of the week were announced, I was number three in the entire United States. It was a great feeling to know I could still do it after not working in the field for ten years. And our plan accomplished its mission as a terrific morale booster for the sale force.

The best executives in every industry understand that the speed of the leader is the speed of the gang. IBM executives, for example, spend time traveling with salespeople, visiting customers in the field. And IBM takes it one step further: senior vice presidents are assigned to work personally with three or four key customers. Not only does this keep them in touch with customers' needs, it assures the sales force that management understands what's happening in the field. This way, nobody makes decisions from some ivory tower.

Of course, you don't have to be an executive at a giant corporation to follow this example. The successful owner of a beauty shop will cut and style hair just as the other hairstylists do. A restaurateur will pitch in to bus tables when diners are waiting to be seated. And a retail executive might be found waiting on customers during the hectic Christmas season.

Managers who roll up their sleeves to work beside their employees send a powerful message. And they set a pace that encourages superior performance.

A MATTER OF PRIDE

Many years ago, during a Christmas holiday snowstorm, my children were getting restless from being indoors for several consecutive days. To make matters worse, the television set went out. In desperation, I picked a repair-shop name from the yellow pages, called the shop, and, to my surprise, a repairman was immediately dispatched to my home.

He climbed over my three children and their toys, rolled up his sleeves, and went to work. Pretty soon, spare television parts were spread across the floor. About an hour later, he had reassembled everything, and he called for me to come in from the kitchen.

I was expecting to be handed a bill, but instead, he asked, "What do you think, ma'am?"

"Looks great," I answered. "How much do I owe you?"

Instead of presenting me with an invoice, he kept staring at the set, admiring his work. "Say, that *is* a great picture," he said. Taking out a bottle of cleaning spray, he cleaned the glass. He stood back again, then walked over to the set and carefully removed a speck of dust with his handkerchief. From that day on, I never called any other television repairman. I liked him because he took such pride in his work. Anytime there was a problem with the set, I'd say to one of the kids, "We had better call up Mr. Bryan."

Pride isn't something that one effortlessly owns. It must be earned. Unfortunately, pride has disappeared from many American workplaces. In days long past, a person took great pride in owning a nice house or car, having a job that provided for the family, and being an American. Unhappily, our society has changed. For some people, too much affluence has taken the sparkle out of having nice things. So has the opposite of affluence; people on welfare can become accustomed to handouts and lose their self-esteem. Today, street people beg for change in every major city across the nation. Loss of harmony between management and workers has changed how many people feel about their jobs. Unpopular wars in Korea and Vietnam, coupled with fraudulent acts committed by government officials, have taken a heavy toll on America's faith in its leaders.

All these changes mean corporate America cannot take proud and loyal workers for granted. Simply providing employment and paying wages will not create an industrious, contented work force. Maintaining an inspired work force that takes pride in its work requires considerably more. People must be managed with respect. This entails always treating both employees and customers fairly and in good faith. A company that makes false promises or markets shoddy merchandise is not worthy of its people's loyalty. And for the same reason, it cannot expect its workers to take pride in their work.

On the contrary, a company has to *earn* a loyal and self-respecting workforce. People will be proud to work for a company that treats them well and creates products and services of value. They then have reason to hold their heads high and be devoted employees.

Once again, I refer to the importance of managing a company by the Golden Rule. At Mary Kay Cosmetics, this means winning loyalty and instilling pride on an everyday basis. We apply this ongoing process across the board—both internally and externally—to our people and our customers. Our actions consistently deliver a message: "We care about you." Recipients of this care can't help developing a strong sense of pride.

chapter 17

HAVING A SENSE OF HUMOR

*T*HERE ARE six reasons why a woman buys something:

1. Because her husband says she can have it.
2. Because her husband says she can't have it.
3. Because it will make her look thinner.
4. Because nobody else has one.
5. Because everybody has one.
6. Just because!

I can't imagine writing a book on priorities without including a chapter on sense of humor. Sometimes we must rely on humor to get us through the day. Humor also helps us put difficulties in the proper perspective, so that we don't take ourselves too seriously.

There are as many different views of humor as there are people. Although a majority of us enjoy a good chuckle, no one really knows what makes us laugh. As E. B. White once said, "Analyzing humor is like dissecting a frog. Few people are interested, and the frog dies of it."

Still, anyone who knows me well understands how much I value a sense of humor. I enjoy laughter!

When properly executed, humor adds a nice touch to almost any situation, business or otherwise. But a note of caution: Timing is everything. Used inappropriately, humor can be disastrous. So use it with discretion. And a good rule of thumb is: When in doubt, don't!

You can also overdo the use of humor. Worse, you can *think* you are funny—and be a minority of one. Making other people laugh is not easy. Perhaps a few hundred people in the United States actually make a good living purely from being funny. And only a handful make it big. Those are not good odds.

I am not trying to discourage anyone from having a sense of humor, because this possession is truly one of the joys of life. I do, however, want you to understand where, when, and how to use it effectively.

WHAT'S FUNNY?

What makes me laugh may not tickle your funny bone. Humor is an individual matter.

How many times has someone told a joke that didn't even make you crack a smile, while those around you exploded with laughter? Have you ever walked out in the middle of a comic play or movie that received rave reviews not only from the critics but from your friends?

Answers to the question of what makes people laugh run the gamut. As children, we laugh at silliness, and most of us continue to find humor in trivial absurdities as adults. Most people laugh at the ridiculous. Some find humor in other people's misfortunes, perhaps because they're relieved these dilemmas aren't their own. Some people find sarcasm funny, and others go beyond that when they are amused by sadistic humor.

Shock also makes us laugh. This may explain why a stand-up comedian can use vulgar language and insult his audience, and yet they laugh. Apparently, even rudeness can be humorous.

There's also humor in irony. To understand irony, think of the man who buys a suit with two pair of pants and then burns a hole in the coat.

Wit also makes us chuckle. Like other forms of humor, it's subjective; what's amusingly perceptive to one person may not be to another. At its best, wit is dry and subtle. Generally, the response to good wit is a slight wriggle of the lips; nevertheless, a witty remark may be thoroughly appreciated and enjoyed.

BREAKING THE ICE

When properly executed, humor is a good way to break the ice with people. We may use levity when we're first introduced to someone as well to relax others in a stressful situation. Generally, injecting humor into tense circumstances lets others know that you do not consider yourself an adversary or, at the very least, that you are in a friendly mood. This is a particularly good message to convey to another party prior to entering negotiations.

Everyone is familiar with the stereotypical traveling salesman who starts off his pitch with a round of jokes. Some say customers have become so accustomed to this routine that they now expect to be entertained before getting down to business. The ritual is based on the belief that humor creates a friendly atmosphere, conducive to overcoming a buyer's resistance.

One reason humor serves as an excellent icebreaker is that it can establish friendly common grounds between two parties. For example, let's say two groups of businesspeople and their attorneys assemble to negotiate a deal. A subtle injection of humor can ease tension and put both sides in a nonantagonistic mood; they can then work together for their mutual benefit. When this is accomplished, everybody is able to walk away from the bargaining table a winner.

Have you noticed that a good public speaker's opening remarks typically contain a joke or a funny story? This helps the audience to feel that the speaker is one of them, that he or she shares some perspective or experience with them.

An example of an opening remark that gets a sizable chuckle is, "It generally takes me two weeks to write a good impromptu speech."

Such icebreakers warm an audience up and make people listen more carefully so they won't miss something funny.

In a speech, put your humor in the context of your message. If your joke, however funny, has no relationship to your subject, the audience feels confused. So you must tie in your humor with your topic.

In my opening remarks at our 1994 Seminar in Dallas, I told a story about a Texas cowboy driving his pickup down the highway with a pig in the front seat. A state trooper stopped him and asked, "What are you doing with that pig on the front seat of your pickup?"

"Well, I found him, and I didn't know what to do with him."

"I'll tell you what to do with him," the state trooper said in a harsh voice. "You take that pig to the zoo."

"Good idea! I'll do that."

The next day, the same cowboy driving the same pickup with the same pig still on the front seat was stopped by the same state trooper.

"I thought I told you to take that pig to the zoo!" said the annoyed policeman.

"Oh, I did," replied the cowboy. "And he had so much fun, today we're going to Six Flags."

This story was a great lead-in to the "Deep in the Heart"(of Texas) theme of our 1994 Seminar.

Most of my jokes relate to my topic, but on occasion I hear one that's so cute, I tell it just to help keep my audience with me. For example, there's a story about a woman who bought an expensive parrot in a pet store.

"He's guaranteed to talk a blue streak, ma'am," the shop-keeper told her.

However, once the woman had taken it home, the parrot let out a streak of profanity. "Look here!" she exclaimed. "We don't allow that kind of talk in this house. Don't you ever talk like that around here again!"

As soon as she turned her back, the parrot began the profanity again. "I guess you didn't understand," she said. "That language is not permitted, and now I'll have to teach you a lesson. I'm going to put you in the freezer for ten minutes. That'll cool you off."

Ten minutes later, she took the poor little parrot out. "Now do you understand?" she asked. "No more profanity. Do you have any questions?"

"Just one," the shivering parrot said. "What did that turkey in there say?"

I always come prepared with a few spare one-liners I can use if needed, according to the mood of my audience. They liven things up and can fit anywhere in my speech. For instance, "Some people get gray, others get blond."

Another time, I might say, "Did you know there are three stages of man: youth, middle age, and 'You're looking great!'" So I don't show partiality, I'll follow up with the four stages of being female: "When a women is under fourteen, she needs good parents. From fourteen to forty, she needs good health. From forty to sixty, she needs personality. And after sixty, I'm here to tell you that what she needs is cash!"

One of my favorite after-dinner stories is about Daniel in the lions' den. "Please understand, this story is not according to the Scripture," I begin. "Have you ever heard about Daniel in the lions' den? When Daniel was put in the lions' den, one by one, the ferocious lions approached to devour him, and each time, he whispered something into the lion's ear. This caused each lion to become very docile and stroll back to a corner to lie down. So, all the lions were obedient and passive.

"Frustrated, his captors removed Daniel from the den and demanded: 'What in the world were you telling those lions?'

"Daniel replied, 'Well, nothing really. I just told them they would be expected to say a few words after dinner.'"

A TOUCH OF WIT

John Kennedy and Richard Nixon were neck and neck in the 1960 presidential campaign when they began the country's first televised debates. It was those debates that tipped the scale in favor of Kennedy. Historians have since credited Kennedy's wit as a conclusive factor. He charmed the nation with his wit. Noticeably missing from the debate was Nixon's sense of humor. In contrast, he was dreadfully serious.

Running for President of the United States is, of course, serious business. Of the many important attributes required to be President, wit shouldn't rank high on the list. Nonetheless, cleverness influences people. To many, wit is synonymous with wisdom. This may be taking it too far. As Voltaire said, "A witty saying proves nothing."

Still, if an individual's witticisms can play a role in determining who will lead the most powerful nation on the planet, wit indubitably influences people on less significant matters. In public speaking, for example, most audiences want more than information. They want to be entertained as well. It is not enough for a speaker to deliver the facts; he or she must present them in a clever and entertaining way in order to win the audience. As a consequence, many professional speakers work hard at being witty. They spend hours practicing the humorous material stored in their arsenal of one-liners, and they perfect their delivery so that their banter sounds spontaneous. Their performance as actors makes them appear to have wit—which is also a fine talent.

Off the stage and in the real world, wit is something you either have or you don't. As someone once said, you can pretend to be serious, but you can't pretend to be witty.

A final caution about wit: Do not overestimate those who appear to have it. While it is certainly a nice touch, people who possess wit are often given more credit for intelligence than they deserve. Like beauty, wit is only skin-deep. Go past the wit and judge people by their character.

A MATTER OF TASTE

When in doubt about whether your humor is in good taste, you're probably wise to keep quiet. Remember, there is sometimes a thin line between being funny and being offensive. If you think there's a chance you might offend someone, recognize that you have far more to lose than to gain by trying to be funny at this moment.

In particular, don't tell jokes that could potentially be hurtful to a member of a minority ethnic group. Even when you think your humor is only in fun, don't risk having someone react negatively. The consequences of insulting someone are far greater than the consequences of amusing someone. After all, people forget funny jokes, but they will certainly remember a racist or sexist remark. Also, a hard-and-fast rule is: There is no place for off-color jokes or profanity.

Another thing to remember is that not all humor transcends culture. What's funny to a Texan, for instance, might not be amusing to a Mexican who lives just across the border. Furthermore, a region's colloquialisms may not be understood by those outside the region.

A friend of mine told a joke to a group of visiting Japanese businesspeople:

"My wife and I were dining out the other night, and my wife asked the waiter, 'Do you serve crabs?' "

"The waiter replied, 'Yes, we serve everybody.' "

My friend explained to me, "There was silence. The joke had no meaning to my Japanese associates, and I had an awkward feeling afterward." Of course, we have all felt embarrassed when one of our jokes bombed, and sometimes it can't be avoided. But as a general rule, use humor sparingly with those from other cultures.

LIGHTEN UP

Many people fail to see the humorous side of life, and consequently endure unnecessary stress. Oftentimes, situations that border on being catastrophic are actually rather amusing—later. Admittedly, you might have to look hard for something funny, but, if you do, chances are you'll find it.

One such instance happened the first time I was profiled on the TV program "60 Minutes," in 1979. On Memorial Day, the producer called to announce that a crew would be at my home early the next morning. Believe me, when you know

"60 Minutes" is coming to your home, you see your living room in an entirely different light! So, like any woman would, I started to inspect my living room very, very carefully.

Seconds later, I exclaimed to Mel, "My goodness, look at the nicks on that baseboard. The housekeeper must have done that with the vacuum. We've got to do something!"

Mel told me not to worry about it. "Nobody will notice it," he insisted.

"Mel, help me find some of the paint the painter left," I pleaded. "I just want to do some minor touching up."

A little while later, he had a quart of yellow paint and some turpentine to clean the brushes. Believe it or not, I took out a cosmetic lip brush—the only brush I could find—dipped it in the paint, and started to touch up the baseboard. Meanwhile, Mel had taken out the vacuum to clean the carpet. Unfortunately, using the vacuum was not what you'd call his specialty. He knocked over the quart of paint right in the middle of the living room carpet! It was horrendous. Frantically, I poured the turpentine on the spilled paint, but it only made the carpet squishy.

"Mel, please see if you can get some more turpentine. Even if it *is* Memorial Day, some place must be open. Get a gallon!"

He went flying out the door and returned shortly with some paint thinner. We poured the whole gallon on the carpet. After ruining my hands, staining my clothes, and using up every rag in the house, we finally got the carpet looking somewhat better—though it was still squishy.

The camera crews arrived bright and early the next morning, and where do you think those folks set up their camera? You guessed it. Right in the middle of the squish. "It sure does smell funny in here," one of them said.

And I thought, "You should have smelled it before I used those three cans of Glade!"

245

Then, in the middle of some shooting a couple of days later, my refrigerator stopped making ice. It was midmorning, and I had just returned from my office. As I walked in the door, the associate producer greeted me by announcing, "We've had a little problem."

Instead of making ice, the refrigerator was spewing water. Water was gushing out, and none of us had any idea how to stop it.

"Has anybody called someone to fix it?" I asked.

"No," they said in unison as somebody handed me the yellow pages.

I found a full-page ad for kitchen appliance repair that read, "twenty-four hours," with "EMERGENCY" printed in bold letters. "Please come over immediately," I said.

"We'll be able to get to it on Friday," the man replied.

"I can't wait two days!" I exclaimed. "My kitchen will be a swimming pool by then. This is an emergency!"

"Sorry, lady, we won't be able to get there until Friday."

The associate producer said, "Give me the phone."

"Hello, this is '60 Minutes,' " she began. Ten minutes later, the repair people were there.

By the afternoon, the refrigerator was fixed and we were rolling again. By the end of the day, everyone was laughing about the incident. "I bet this is a first for '60 Minutes,' " I said.

Once everything was under control, a camaraderie developed between the network crew and the rest of us. We seemed more unified, as if the near disaster had brought us together.

Later, when the crew began packing up the cameras, the assistant producer said, "We'd like to shoot you in action. What's coming up soon on your agenda?"

Thinking I'd discourage them, I said, "Oh, in eighteen days, I'll be addressing a group of two thousand women in Canada."

"Where in Canada?"

"At the Harbour Castle in Toronto," I answered.

I thought that would be the last I'd see of "60 Minutes," but when I stepped off the plane in Toronto, there they were: the "60 Minutes" camera crew was filming me! They continued to film me all the way from the airport to the hotel and that evening at our "guest night."

To my chagrin, the hotel's air-conditioning was broken. It was summer and ninety degrees in the ballroom. When two thousand people assembled in the room, the temperature must have exceeded the one hundred-degree mark.

National Sales Director Anne Newbury and I were the two principal speakers that night, and we were perspiring so much, all our makeup had vanished. I thought, " '60 Minutes' is here, and we want to make a good impression on all these people. What are they going to think of us? How are we ever going to get through this night?"

But rather than panicking, Anne and I went through our entire presentation as if nothing was the matter—although we made a few jokes about the heat and the vanishing makeup. Meanwhile, as we looked our worst in front of a live audience of two thousand women, I kept thinking about the millions of viewers who would see us on "60 Minutes."

At the end of that long evening, the producer came over and shook my hand saying, "Mary Kay, I just wanted to tell you that I think you are one super lady."

When I heard those words, I breathed a sigh of relief because I knew he was the man who wields the editing scissors. If he was in our corner, perhaps we wouldn't look so bad on national television after all. As it turned out, our segment on "60 Minutes" was received well and generated a lot of positive publicity for the company. Two years later, when it was replayed, our sales had quadrupled and our number of consultants had tripled.

If there is a lesson to be learned from this trying experience, it is: Don't let problems that are out of your control get to you. Instead of panicking, look at the humorous side. Doing this will help to keep things in their proper perspective.

Every woman should attempt to do this, no matter how stressed out she may feel as she attempts to make her career gel with her personal life. I understand the anxiety you may feel when things aren't going your way. And how well I understand the pressures you constantly feel because of demands on your time! There simply aren't enough hours in the day to attend to your family, much less to spend a few minutes alone.

Even so, we must learn to lighten up. We have to take life in stride, one step at a time. As long as we can laugh and stop treating difficulties as disasters, everything will be just fine.

chapter 18

YES, YOU CAN!

THE HIGHLIGHT of our annual Seminar is Awards Night. On this special evening, no expense is spared to create elaborate staging and glamour to rival a Cecil B. DeMille production. During this event, our top performers are rewarded with the fabulous prizes that have made Mary Kay Cosmetics synonymous with luxury and glamour. This is the night when dazzling diamonds and dream vacations are presented, and deserving queens are called to center stage to be crowned for their outstanding achievements.

During the evening, I remind every woman in the audience that she can be on center stage next year. She can experience the joy and pride of this year's queens. "What does she have that *you* can't have fixed?" I challenge. "Next year it could be you who is on center stage. *You can do it!*"

Mary Kay Seminar is the ultimate expression of a simple concept in which we believe with all our hearts: We can praise people to success! We keep people aware of how we appreciate them and their performance. And how do they respond? They respond by doing even better! Through praise and encouragement, I have seen thousands of women soar to heights they never imagined they could reach.

THE MAGIC OF BELIEVING

I will never forget one particular Monday morning during the early days of my sales career. As I usually did at the beginning of each week, I phoned to confirm appointments that I had booked the previous week. After being informed that Monday's appointments had all been canceled, I tried to juggle my schedule for the week so I could get in some sales calls later that day. By midmorning, everything I had scheduled for the entire week was canceled!

I was in the depths of depression. At the time, I lived paycheck to paycheck. If I didn't sell that week, my three children and I didn't eat. Not knowing what to do, I picked up a book someone had given me. It was Napoleon Hill's *Think and Grow Rich*. I didn't have time to read the entire book at one sitting, so I decided to concentrate on one chapter a week; I'd read each chapter over the course of seven days, so I could put into action what I had read. There were fifteen chapters, and by the end of the fifteen-week period, my sales and my self-esteem had increased substantially. What a difference that book made in my life!

I recommend Claude Bristol's *The Magic of Believing* as another wonderful motivational book. A former newspaper reporter, Bristol offers his observations on people he interviewed during his journalism career, when he wrote about individuals who were either ill, recovering from illness, or dying. And he notes that certain football teams win, while other teams, just as skilled, lose. After lengthy research, he concludes, "In time, I discovered a golden thread that makes life work. That thread can be named in a single word—*belief!*" Bristol's studies convinced him that people with belief can do fantastic things.

When you are consumed with strong belief, all that you desire comes within your reach. Again I refer to Napoleon

Hill's famous quotation: "Whatever the mind can conceive and believe, it can achieve." I have complete faith in those words. You must remember that every great achievement started out as an idea in someone's mind.

DREAMS CAN COME TRUE,
IT CAN HAPPEN TO YOU!

Everyone needs to have a dream, something beyond easy grasp. Contrary to what many people think, happiness is not the acquisition of wealth. I understand the preoccupation people tend to have with money. They think if they were rich, their financial problems would evaporate and they'd have no worries. Having been poor, I understand this way of thinking. It's hard to be content when you can't pay your bills and you are working day and night to make ends meet. But once you reach the point when you have enough money to cover the necessities, earning even more doesn't necessarily sustain happiness. This is obvious each time we read about a rich person in the entertainment industry who accidentally overdoses on drugs or commits suicide. Despite the satisfaction of every material want, that life evidently had a void.

How can people appear to have everything, and yet be discontent? Perhaps they have stopped dreaming. I believe each of us needs to have a reason to get up each morning. We need something to anticipate—something that excites us. A truly happy person is someone who never quite reaches the rainbow's end. I have enjoyed so much during my lifetime—far more than I ever dreamed possible. Still, I find it difficult to wait for the sun to come up on each new day. This is because I continue to have exciting prospects. Every day of my life, I thank God for giving me such happiness.

Having a dream is actually better than reaching its fulfill-ment. Weren't there times in your life when you had looked forward to something for a long time, but when you finally obtained it, you felt let down? Think back to the anticipation of getting your driver's license. Or what about your high school diploma, first car, or first house? Oftentimes the excite-ment that leads up to a faraway vacation, a big dinner party, or a friend's wedding is followed by a letdown, because the actual event doesn't live up to your expectations.

Always being able to look forward to something special is one of life's great pleasures. The dream itself may be what makes the journey most interesting. As Kahlil Gibran said, "The significance of a man is not in what he attains but rather in what he longs to attain." So go ahead and dream—have wonderful dreams—and as you attain those dreams, keep right on raising your sights, striving for even greater heights.

Having someone to share your dream makes it even better. Involve your husband and children in your dreams. Tell them of your desires; let them be a part of your aspirations. I did this with my children, and even when they were very young, they worked with me to make "our" dream come true.

YOU CAN DO IT!

At the beginning of this book, I described how my mother would encourage me by saying, "Mary Kay, you can do it!" Now, as a mother wants the best for her child, I want to give other women the opportunities that were denied me as a young woman.

My career has been described as a rags-to-riches story. I had to pull myself up by my bootstraps. It took God a long time to prepare me for the job He had for me. All my years of experience—mixed with trial and error, marked by set-backs and disappointments—were necessary before God could guide me to form Mary Kay Cosmetics. By no stretch of the imagination has my life been an overnight success story.

Today, thousands of women in the world of Mary Kay Cosmetics have achieved enormous success. Many individuals joined our ranks with low self-esteem and, at first, set limited goals for themselves. Some wanted only to supplement their family's earnings with some extra money each week. As these women enjoyed initial small successes, accompanied by praise and encouragement, they set more ambitious goals, and still more ambitious ones after that. In time, the "you-can-do-it" message came through to them loud and clear. They believed in themselves and perceived no limits on what they could accomplish.

Women have come a long way and our earnings are moving upward, although they must rise farther before our pay equals that of men. We have made tremendous headway in some professions. As I've mentioned before, today in the United States, as many women as men are enrolled in schools of law, medicine, and dentistry. It is our duty now to make sure women all over the world receive equal opportunity.

Now that women are able to pursue fulfilling careers, we are presented with new challenges. We must figure out how to remain good wives and good mothers while triumphing in the workplace. This is no easy task for the woman who works full-time. There are only so many hours in each day. To prosper in your career and spend sufficient time with your husband and children, you must prioritize. From time to time you may choose to place your career on the back burner. This may mean that, at certain times in your life, you may not be able to devote the same amount of time to your career that a man

253

could, or a single, childless woman could—that is, if your family is a higher priority than your job.

As women, we bear the children; this both enriches and complicates our lives. The challenge of juggling all our roles— wife, mother, daughter, sister, friend, career woman—is a significant one, but one that brings with it many rewards. With God's help, every woman can find a way to bring balance into her life—no matter how great the obstacles.

Remember that when God closes a door, He always opens a window. As we say at Mary Kay Cosmetics: Expect great things and great things will happen. Around here, we are realists—realists who expect a miracle every day. Your God-given womanhood, intuition, and desire to nurture make you His living miracle.

You can have anything in this world if you want it badly enough and are willing to pay the price. With your priorities in order, press on, and never look back. May all of your dreams come true. You can, indeed, have it all!

Index

255

256